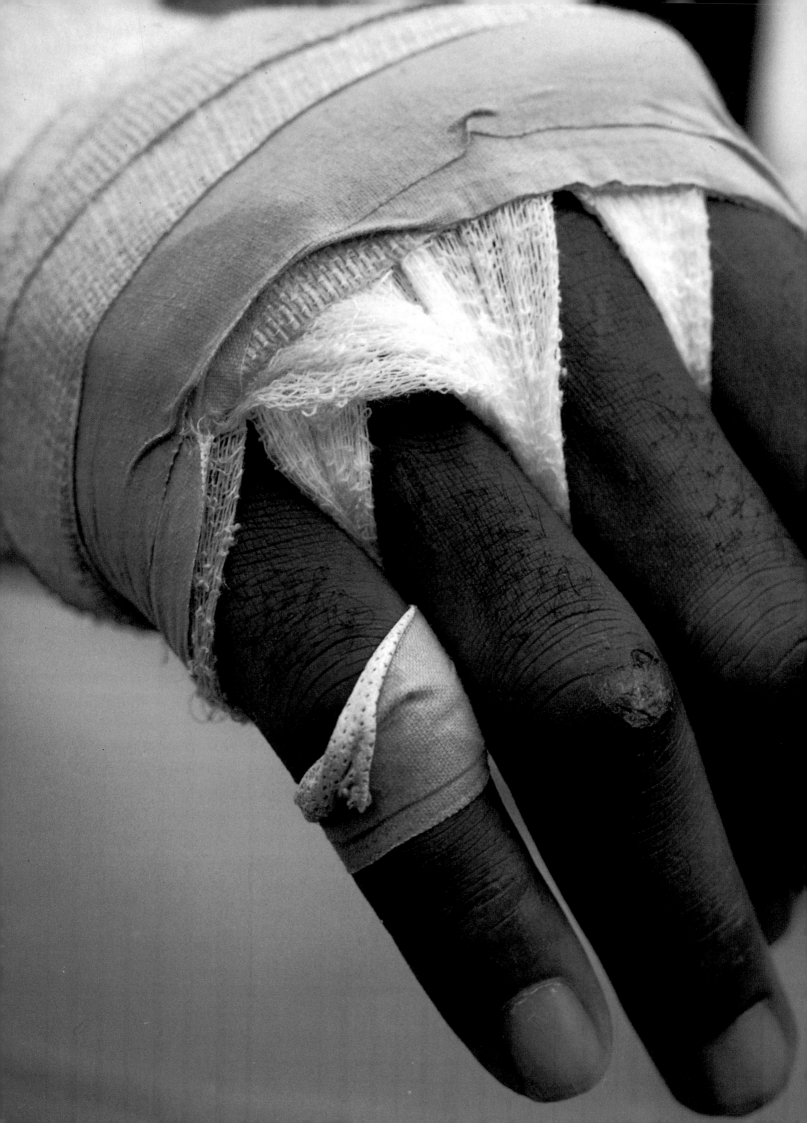

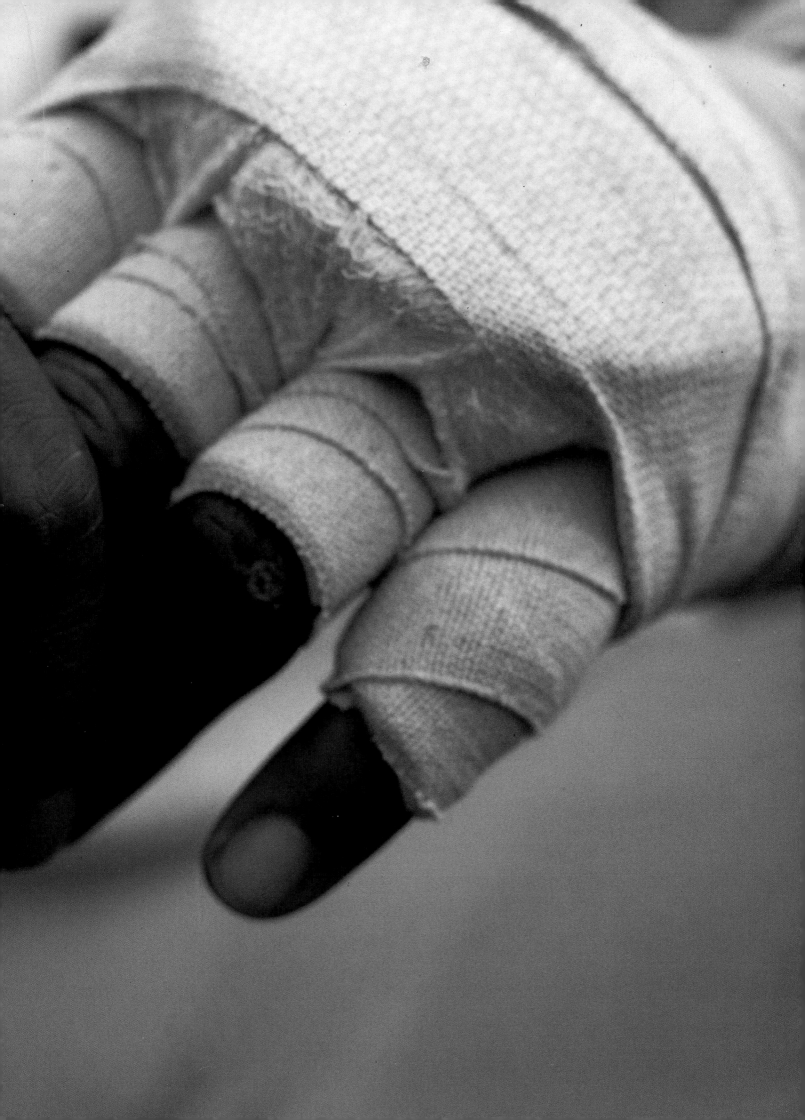

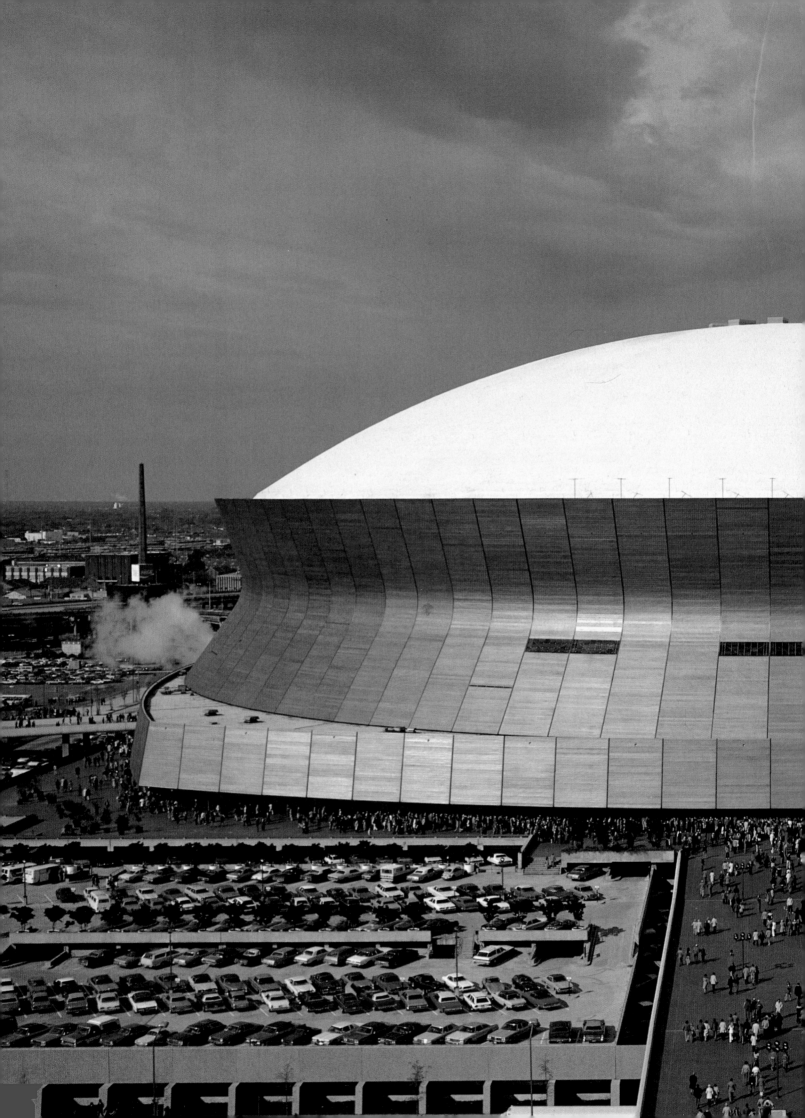

FOOTBALL

PHOTOGRAPHS BY
Walter Iooss, Jr.

TEXT BY
Dan Jenkins

Harry N. Abrams, Inc., Publishers, New York

Page 1: Kids' football at a farm outside Pella, Iowa

Pages 2–3: I told Jack Tatum and John Matuszak to look at me "like you want to take my head off." December 1979. Oakland–Alameda County Coliseum, Oakland

Pages 4–5: Browns wide receiver Dave Logan beats cornerback Mel Blount and makes a one-handed scoring catch. November 1979. Cleveland Stadium

Pages 6–7: The hands of L. C. Greenwood, Steeler left end. Unwrapped, his fingers could wear four Super Bowl rings. July 1973

Pages 8–9: When I awoke in my New Orleans hotel room the day of Super Bowl XII and opened the curtains, I saw what looked like a gigantic flying saucer. January 15, 1978. Louisiana Superdome, New Orleans

Pages 10–11: This may have been the best single day I've ever had as a football photographer. There are four pictures in the book from this USC–UCLA game. November 1976. Los Angeles Memorial Coliseum

Pages 12–13: Detroit running back Altie Taylor evades a group of New England defenders. September 26, 1971. Schaefer Stadium, Foxboro, Massachusetts

Pages 14–15: Two hours before this game in Denver, I had been sunbathing in the mountain air. By the fourth quarter, I was in a blizzard with only one working camera, fitted with a 20mm lens. December 1979. Mile High Stadium, Denver

Page 16: The two things I remember most about this game at Cincinnati's Riverfront Stadium in 1976 are how the snow muted the sound of the crowd and how the white blanket turned an artificial setting into a natural wonderland.

Editor: Robert Morton
Designer: Dirk Luykx

Library of Congress Cataloging-in-Publication Data
Iooss, Walter.
Football.
1. Football. 2. Football—Pictorial works.
I. Jenkins, Dan. II. Title.
GV951.I56 1986   796.332   86–3587
ISBN 0–8109–0938–3

Times Mirror Books

Printed and bound in Japan

 Preface

By Walter Iooss, Jr.

The pictures displayed here cover twenty-five years and date back to some of my earliest assignments for *Sports Illustrated.* I was eighteen when some of them were taken. That was also the year I started shooting football for SI, 1962.

I covered more than 300 games during this time. I've endured temperatures from 20 degrees below zero to 120 above, torrential rains, blizzards, fog, and riotous fans. On the other hand, I've enjoyed private Lear jets, chartered helicopters, stretch limos, and hotels from Wink, Texas, to Beverly Hills, California. I covered NFL championships in the sixties with just two other SI photographers (Neil Leifer and James Drake). I've also covered a Super Bowl in Pasadena (1979) with eleven others. I went several times to a game called the Runner-up Bowl, which I thought of as the Fiasco Bowl, but it was played in Miami in January, so I never missed it.

I remember fall seasons played on grass under a God-given sky when I was able to shoot from the real sideline of the field, not the one six to twelve feet back that now keeps the hordes of press, photographers, and TV people away from the field. And I can recall games when I could hardly keep the film in my cameras between plays because there was no such thing as a TV time-out. Now there seem to be more time-outs than good plays at some games.

On a fall day in 1962 I went to photograph my first pro game outside the New York–New Jersey area where I had grown up and was beginning to work. I took the train to Baltimore to see my beloved Colts. (They had become beloved to me after the 1958 sudden death game that Dan Jenkins writes about elsewhere in this book.) Knowing that I would be on the sidelines, I wore light-colored clothes that Sunday so that I might see myself more clearly later on my favorite TV show, *Pro-Football Highlights,* which was broadcast in black and white at that time.

The game was won by Baltimore when Jimmy Orr made an incredible catch, bobbling the ball as he fell into the end zone for a touchdown. The play happened so close to me that I had to run back from the sidelines, focusing over my shoulder, because I had a 180mm lens on my camera. I took one frame. Then I ran toward Orr, and in my excitement started to leap up and down, patting him on the back. Forgotten was the fact that I thought I had missed the shot.

Next Thursday I watched *Pro-Football Highlights* and there I was, a frenzied photographer

pounding Orr's back after his great catch. The single photograph, which I hadn't missed after all, is shown above. It is one of my favorites.

I would like to thank certain people who have helped make my career and who have given me a wonderful life: my mother, who didn't want me to be a photographer but stuck by me when I most needed her; my father, who believed in my talent when there was no other; my wife, Eva, and sons, Christian and Bjorn, who have given me their love and support and a beautiful home.

George Bloodgood, my first SI picture editor, gave me my start and stuck with me through my learning years in the sixties—which had to be difficult. My longtime friend, assistant, confidant, and sports expert, Mike Ehret, traveled with me on many of these assignments.

Introduction

By Dan Jenkins

I'm not exactly sure how others go about it, but getting myself born and raised in Fort Worth, Texas, made it easy for me to become a football junkie. I think I might have been a football junkie before I was even a kid, before I knew how to sidestep a kitchen table, stiff-arm a lamp, and throw a bullet pass into the waiting arms of a living room sofa.

Down there in the old hometown, in the land of the chicken fried steak, we had this football team called TCU (Texas Christian University) and TCU was hot stuff in the 1930s, which is when I was trying to grow up. It's partly because of the TCU Horned Frogs, I'm sure, that the thirties are still my favorite decade. Everything was better in the thirties. Movies, gangsters, convertibles, trains, *food,* platinum blondes, drugstores, comic books, the radio, parents. Well, everything except air conditioning.

Anyhow, it was in the thirties that these big, white-jerseyed TCU Horned Frogs with a purple stripe down the backs of their shiny khaki pants used to beat up on all of the other football teams regularly.

You have to understand what these victories meant. The TCU Horned Frogs were bringing national recognition to our city. And Fort Worth didn't enjoy much national recognition in those days unless Bonnie Parker and Clyde Barrow knocked off another bank or shot another motorcycle cop and were known to be hiding out in one of the cowboy hotels near the stockyards.

When I would sit around the supper table at home with a full complement of granddads, uncles, and cousins, I would be fed TCU's first All-American quarterback, Slingin' Sam Baugh, for an entree—along with whatever else I might want in the way of country sausage, biscuits and gravy, or the drumstick of a chicken somebody had chased down in our backyard and fried.

And then for dessert I would be fed TCU's next All-American quarterback, Davey O'Brien, along with peach cobbler and homemade ice cream.

What was not, as they say, to like? What Great Depression?

At the age of seven I remember the granddads, uncles, and cousins getting very excited and even semiarrogant. The year was 1935 and Slingin' Sam Baugh was turning the TCU Horned Frogs into the No. 1 team in the nation. It said so right there in the newspapers.

It was explained to me what a big deal this was. Always in the past, the scientific professors who decided such things had chosen legendary schools like Notre Dame, Southern Cal, Princeton, Michigan, Pitt, Yale, Army, and Navy. But now it was us, by damn.

Then I remember the granddads, uncles, and cousins getting even more excited and totally arrogant in 1938 when Davey O'Brien turned TCU into the No. 1 team in the country *again*. I was ten. The AP poll was three.

Small wonder I chose to ignore the unexcited and usually unemployed uncle who would say, "Can't nobody make a living in this chicken-squat town." I was certain I lived in the football capital of the universe and felt sorry for anybody who didn't.

The relatives would take me to the games to see Sam Baugh and Davey O'Brien in person. I would watch with awe as TCU lined up in a Double Wing or Triple Wing or Spread Formation, what they call the Shotgun today, like it's a brainy invention of the pros. Baugh or O'Brien would be crouched down, elbows on the knees. Then the center would hike the ball, as they used to say, and marvelous things happened. Baugh or O'Brien would spin and dart through the line, or shoot a shovel pass to somebody, or hand the ball off to a flying halfback to launch a double or triple reverse, or they would just fade back and loft a pass, or drill one, or float one, to a rangy, glue-fingered end for a touchdown.

Another thing Sam and Davey did quite often, which seems to have become a lost art, was wriggle through the line for ten yards and then suddenly jump up, whirl around in the air, and fire a long lateral out to the sideline. Waiting there, all alone, would be a reliable halfback like Jimmy Lawrence or Earl Clark. The crowd-pleasing halfback would catch the lateral and speed down the sideline until he was overtaken, whereupon he would toss his own lateral to an escorting line-man, a center like Ki Aldrich, maybe, or a tackle like I. B. Hale, and the lineman would lumber on into the end zone for another touchdown.

It has occurred to me that even linemen had more fun then.

All of these things took place in a concrete bowl that was half sunken into the ground on the TCU campus, a campus that was only a few blocks from my house, and only a fifteen-minute streetcar ride from the picture shows downtown.

That stadium at the time looked to me as if it held at least 500,000 people. It actually seated 30,000.

Another reason I became a football addict was the radio.

Football players were about eight feet tall on the radio, and they could outrun a north wind.

It wasn't just the announcers like Bill Stern and Kern Tips who made the football players so big and fast and elusive, and certainly guiltless when it came to being scored upon or even losing a game; it was the imagination.

I'm convinced I saw football games more vividly when I stared into the radio than I ever have on television. On a TV set, football players are only about this big, anyhow. Little old tiny things. And on television, you can plainly see these little old tiny things doing a lot of great big dumb things. They fumble. They slip down. They drop passes. They get caught from behind.

Football players never did any of this on the radio—not in the thirties, at least. A ballcarrier never got tackled unless he was woefully outnumbered and hemmed in by Mongol hordes. He never fumbled unless the ball was jarred loose by the most bone-rattling blow you could envision. He might slip down on occasion but only if the field was a virtual quagmire. And he never dropped a pass. He might fail to catch a pass now and then, but only for a very good reason. He would have been forced to make this suicidal dive for the ball and it was just out of reach.

The radio is responsible for the fact that I still think of Texas A&M's Jarrin' John Kimbrough as being only slightly smaller than a redwood tree and fully capable of caroming through a steel door.

Kimbrough was the line-wrecking fullback who replaced Baugh and O'Brien in my heart and scrapbook after Sam and Davey were gone. Jarrin' John immediately led the Texas Aggies to the national title of 1939, which made it comforting for me to know that the State of Texas was still the football capital of the universe, even if Fort Worth no longer was.

Kimbrough caromed a lot on the radio. I don't know if any fullback ever caromed as much as Kimbrough caromed. Frankly, I had to wonder at times if some of his caroming was really necessary. I mean, if you were as big and strong as he was, why wouldn't you just blast your way into the end zone? Why fool around with caroming?

Jarrin' John was actually 6′ 2″ and weighed 215 pounds.

That is not a big person these days. I have been 6′ 2″ and 215 pounds when I put my mind to it. But it was big in the thirties, let me tell you, and the day I saw Kimbrough carom all over TCU Stadium—and TCU's football team—he seemed to be the biggest and caromingest individual I ever hoped to lay eyes on.

A year later, in 1940, I experienced something while listening to the radio that made me realize I was smarter than everybody else in the family.

Kimbrough, now a senior, was caroming his way to another All-American season at A&M, and the Aggies had been the No. 1 team in the polls all year. It seemed likely that the Aggies were going to repeat as national champions and surely be invited to the Rose Bowl. All they needed to do was beat the University of Texas in their last game on Thanksgiving Day.

Naturally, the whole family assembled to listen to the game on the radio.

Everybody knew the Aggies were supposed to win the game by three or four touchdowns—everybody but the Texas Longhorns, apparently. With a keen, triple-threat back named Pete Layden and a little rocket named Cowboy Jack Crain doing something wonderful, Texas took a 7–0 lead in the game's first 58 seconds. This was, by the way, a better Texas team than anyone had figured. Virtually the same guys came back the following year to make the Longhorns No. 1 in the nation. Hey, listen. Those were high times for the Southwest Conference.

But back to the radio. I didn't like to hear that the Aggies were trailing in this all-important game, and the longer they trailed by the same score of 7–0, the angrier and more disillusioned I became.

Meanwhile, all of the granddads and uncles and cousins were enjoying it, whooping it up for the gigantic upset that seemed more and more inevitable.

"Teach them Aggies to act snooty," said an uncle, who must have known some snooty Aggies and didn't remember acting so snooty himself when TCU was No. 1.

"Hell, they just army, is all they are," said a cousin, referring to the fact that Texas A&M was a one hundred percent military school in those years.

"March on *that*," said a granddad when Jarrin' John Kimbrough had neglected to carom again.

I applied all the body English I could, and slammed into all of the pillows and chairs that I could, as the Aggies spent what seemed like six or seven hours inside the Texas 10-yard line, but A&M never scored. They lost the game, 7–0, *and* the national championship, *and* the Rose Bowl bid, and I was sick about it. That's when I knew I was smarter than everybody else.

Why hadn't the stupid, short-sighted Texas Longhorns had the intelligence to lose the damn game for the good of the state and the good of the conference? What we had at stake here was regional pride. So why was everybody in the house pulling for the idiot Longhorns to mess things up? Now look who was going to win the national championship—Minnesota! The Minnesota Golden Gophers, the same evil swine that had beaten the glamorous Tom Harmon and the elegant Michigan Wolverines, who only had the best-looking helmets in the world and didn't deserve to lose to a bunch of drab, dreary Gopher-Swedes. Where was Minnesota, anyhow? Up there in Alaska, wasn't it?

Football is how I first learned that life wasn't going to make any sense sometimes.

As for the third and last reason for my being a football junkie before I was old enough to smoke, I come to still pictures, the pictures of the gridiron heroes that appeared in the newspapers and magazines.

There were two kinds of football pictures taken back then. There were the posed pictures, which were the contorted bodies you could study while you listened to the games on the radio; and there were the action pictures, which confirmed that the games had, in fact, been played.

The posed publicity shots tried to stress action, too. Ballcarriers sneered as they lifted a knee and stiff-armed a phantom tackler. Passers stuck out their tongues and did a leaping split as they cocked their arms. Punters poked their legs into the sky, higher than a chorus girl ever had, and higher than a punter ever would in a game. Linemen spread their arms and charged into the lens, or dived headfirst for fumbles.

Game-action photos were more exotic. They covered the whole front page of Sunday sports sections, and two or three pages inside. I miss that, the way newspapers used to splash the pictures around. I believe newspapers have let TV con them out of something. There are newspapers that still have the space to do this, but issue-conscious sports editors would rather give us a long, unreadable feature story about a marathon runner who eats seaweed.

Before TV, sports sections endeavored to show you the game you hadn't seen. Newspapers had these trusty artists who would doll up an eight-column picture of a play that had occurred on Saturday. It was rarely a crucial play unless the old Speed Graphic shooter got real lucky. What you would see was a determined Davey O'Brien running with the football through a scattered secondary. And the artist would have drawn a bunch of dots from where the run had originated, and then a curving line to where it had ended. And there would be these names pasted everywhere. "Aldrich Undresses Cole." "Hale Kept Hickey Out." "Hall Handles Eakin." And the overhead caption would read: "Here Comes O'Brien!"

Well, football photography has come a long way, principally because of shooters like Walter Iooss, Jr. I don't say Walter is the greatest sports photographer who ever lived because he's an old friend. I say it because I've been dazzled by his pictures for the past twenty-five years.

In football, Walter knows how to fill a frame with more than football. If the situation calls for violence, he's got it. If it calls for mood, he's got that, too. There's a deeply felt understanding, a poetry, a love for the game in Walter's work. Personally, I don't know where in the devil it comes from because there's a generation gap here. Walter didn't listen to football games on the radio when he was a kid. He listened to the Marvelettes.

Kids

It begins on a familiar patch of ground. The front lawn. The backyard. Maybe the vacant lot next door. Uncle Joe Bob Jim throws a pass. An eight-year-old cradles the ball between his forearms and chest. When the eight-year-old learns to throw it back with a spiral, ecstasy kicks in.

So a game of catch is how it starts. But the older relative is soon replaced by other kids. Huddles start to take shape—in the wheatfields and cornfields of the Midwest, on the prairies of Texas, along the beaches of the West and South, even in the streets of the East and North.

Young quarterbacks quickly assert their qualities of leadership. They draw pass routes in the dirt with Popsicle sticks. Socially, an evolution occurs. Kids who can run, catch, and throw inherit the "skilled" positions. Fat kids and slow kids are assigned the menial tasks of snapping the ball, or getting in somebody's way.

In neighborhood football, there are no double down-and-ins, no Z-42 Blows, no stunting 3-4 defenses. Only a self-appointed quarterback, saying:

"Bubba, you go to the blue Chevy and cut for the fireplug. Eddie Joe, you fake to the flower bed and take off for the cedar tree. Rest of you block. Burrell, if you hup it to me too low again, I'll kick your ass."

In the meantime, many of America's young ladies are learning about eye shadow and practicing kick turns, dreaming of some glittery moment as a UCLA song girl or a Dallas Cowboy cheerleader.

It is one of life's continuing mysteries that pep squads never lose their pep, even under the gloomiest of circumstances.

The high school team can be down by 42 points in the fourth quarter, but on the sideline a cluster of bouncy blondes and brunettes will be chanting:

Tuck in your shirt,
Pull up your pants.
Come on, boys,
You still got a chance!

Maybe it has something to do with the teacher, the demanding woman who always seems to be in charge of the pep squad: Magda Goebbels.

"You're not doing it right, Martha Ann!" the teacher bellows. "Either do it like Susie does it or go to study hall!"

Martha Ann examines Susie with envy. Susie is a siren. All the moves, a hand on her curvy hip. Martha Ann would like to imitate Susie, but something within her won't permit it. What Martha Ann wants to explain to the teacher, although she doesn't know how yet, is that Susie is fourteen, going on thirty—a bimbo ahead of her time.

Elsewhere, Mom has also become involved in football. Mom has learned the hard way that it's best to remove the pads from football pants before washing them. Mom has learned to do grease-stained jerseys by hand. Mom has learned new words for her vocabulary: blitz, wishbone, zone, curl, post, keeper, cornerback.

"Larry, you should have blitzed the keeper when you wishboned the post."

Larry shakes his head wearily.

"Gimme a break, Mom, okay?"

Two paths lead to the stardom of high school, college, and the pros. One requires more imagination. That's the sandlot game. The other requires more discipline. That's organized kiddie football, principally the Pop Warner League, the counterpart of Little League baseball.

Launched back in 1929 by a Philadelphia stockbroker and named for the venerable old coach at Carlisle, Stanford, and Temple University, Pop Warner football now encompasses more than 4,000 teams in thirty-seven states and Mexico, the warriors ranging in age from seven to fourteen.

In organized football, the eight- or ten-year-old may seem bewildered at times, but he'll surely look stylish in his globular helmet and $200 worth of vinyl, polyurethane, and rayon gear.

If the kid likes to "hit," he'll soon find that loyalty, teamwork, and the competitive urge have become built-in character traits.

Along the way, he'll experience many emotions. He'll know what it's like to hear a shrill whistle being blown at him by an ominous figure in a striped shirt. He'll hear muscular coaches yelling at him. And he'll also be swept up in the adoration that flows from the grandstands. Mostly, he'll learn to pick himself up off the ground.

Numerous stars have come out of organized kiddie football. Three of the most notable Pop Warner graduates were Marcus Allen, a legend at USC before he became a legend with the Los Angeles Raiders; Notre Dame's Joe Theismann, who went on to other exploits with the Washington Redskins; and Boston College's Doug Flutie, who, like TCU's Davey O'Brien in another era, refused to let size prevent him from throwing enough touchdown passes to win the Heisman Trophy.

But it's not all streamlined uniforms and the cheers of family and friends if the kid chooses the rigorous road of organized football.

At some point in his teenage years he will undoubtedly have to ask himself if it's truly worth it to hear the following lecture on the sideline from a furious grownup:

"Billy Joe, you ain't got a gut in your body. You've let your team down, your folks down, your coaches down. You've embarrassed the whole community. Now I'm gonna give you one more chance to go in there and hurt somebody, goddammit. And if you don't, you're gonna be runnin' laps and doin' pushups till your pecker drops off!"

Thus, in the grand tradition of American athletic encouragement, men are molded, stars are born.

The College Game

When the Arkansas Razorbacks play football, it's not unusual to see hundreds of adults at the game with pigs on their heads. Not real pigs, of course. The real pigs sit in their laps.

In Baton Rouge, Louisiana, the fans will paint their faces purple and gold—the designer faces of LSU.

At Clemson, South Carolina, you'll see cheeks and foreheads dotted with the tracks of tiger paws. I have observed that when these tracks reach the brain, whoops and howls are accepted as intelligent conversation.

They let out long, loud rumbles of "Roll, Tide, roll" in Alabama.

They shout, "How 'bout them Dawgs?" in Georgia.

And anybody familiar with the University of Texas Longhorns knows what it means when a person displays the index and pinkie finger on one hand. It means the world is supposed to "Hook 'em, Horns!"

College football fans are a society of millions to whom the game is no less important than blood. Because it is the most physical of our athletic games and has often been compared to war by the men who coach it, football touches something deeper than the enthusiasm for mere sport in all of us who like it and follow it.

Okay, call us crazy. We don't care.

The madness began in 1869 when Princeton and Rutgers played the first football game. It wasn't any sort of game like we know today. It was twenty-five guys on a side who removed their waistcoats and played Tug Your Groin.

But even then there were uniforms. The men from Rutgers wore red turbans. Even then there was a football yell. The men of Princeton uttered some vague chant they remembered from a few years earlier when New York's Seventh Regiment had marched through town on its way to that bowl game with the Confederacy.

It took some years for the sport to gain a little sophistication. That happened in 1913 when a couple of student athletes named Knute Rockne and Gus Dorais did a funny thing with the ball and drew attention to the forward pass at a little school hidden among the Indiana sycamores, a place called Notre Dame.

But as I interpret history, I don't believe the fans started to go seriously crazy until the 1920s—after the pioneer era. It was in this giddy decade that writers like Grantland Rice began to immortalize Notre Dame's Four Horsemen—Illinois' Red Grange, Stanford's Ernie Nevers, Army's Chris Cagle—and practically everyone else who wore a leather helmet and high-top shoes.

By then, schools were erecting stadiums to hold 30,000 people, then 50–, then 80–, then 100,000, and the race for No. 1, for the national championship, was on the way to becoming the most romantic, if elusive, of goals. The sport was stitching itself into the fabric of American society, and once there, it would become inseparable.

I know this. Let a school win a big game today—any school—and what you've got on your hands are marauding groups of people babbling incoherently that their boys are tougher than yours, their colors more regal, their coeds prettier, and their campus, city, state, and region the only sensible places to be, or be from.

The madness takes on some bewildering aspects.

It is public knowledge that Auburn built a half-million-dollar aviary to house an American eagle—"War eagle!" is the cry heard through many a hotel lobby—although Auburn's official mascot remains a tiger.

On Strawberry Hill, a slope above California's Memorial Stadium in Berkeley, thousands of bodies are strewn about on the day of a game, some drinking, some sleeping, some playing the flute. In the revolutionary sixties, some even wore clothes.

Put Michigan against Ohio State, either in sold-out Ann Arbor or overflowing Columbus, and invariably some poor soul outside the stadium will hold up a hand-lettered sign that says: "If I don't get a ticket, I'll kill myself!"

In Dallas the night before the Texas Longhorns battle the Oklahoma Sooners in an annual event of the Texas State Fair, the arrests for disturbing the peace average 400 each year.

At the Cotton Bowl the next afternoon, the crowd of 75,000 is always evenly divided. Some Texan is likely to carry a sign that says, "If God hadn't invented dust, there wouldn't be an Oklahoma." "Hook 'em, Fags," an Oklahoman retaliates.

The 80,000 in the Gator Bowl in Jacksonville at the Georgia–Florida game every year are just as loud—and drunker. They rev up all week long with pep rallies, cocktail parties, golf and tennis tournaments, class reunions, and more hollering than you could find in a series of hotel fires.

The colors come out—red and black for the Dawgs, orange and blue for the Gators—among bankers, waitresses, computer analysts, mechanics, lawyers, and so on.

One morning in a Jacksonville cafe six days before the game, a man noticed a waitress wearing an orange skirt, blue blouse, orange boots, and a blue-and-orange cowboy hat.

"Doris," the man asked, "are you already wearin' your Gator Colors?"

"Just two of 'em," the waitress said, slinging a bowl of gravy in the customer's general direction.

Sometimes the Stanford University band, whackiest and most inventive in the land, can get a little out of control in Palo Alto, California.

There was this recent autumn when a San Jose politician got himself arrested on a drunk driving charge. Hearing of it, the Stanford band decided to dedicate a halftime performance to him. Which it did. After the public address announcement, the Stanford band staggered onto the field, swigging from bottles, falling down, pretending to vomit.

One year at a national political convention, a Southern delegate actually stood at a microphone on network television and said, "The great state of Alabama, as proud of this ticket as it is of its No. 1 football team, casts all of its ballots for . . ."

Battles in wartime have been interrupted in order for our generals and admirals to listen to the Army–Navy game on the radio. We know this to be true because of a wire that Army's coach Red Blaik once received.

The year was 1944. It had been a long time since Army had turned out a steamroller. So when Blaik's Black Knights of the Hudson capped off an undefeated and untied season in '44—the first of the Glenn Davis–Doc Blanchard teams—by whipping up on Navy's Midshipmen and insuring West Point of its first poll-vote national championship, the following telegram fell into Blaik's hands:

> THE GREATEST OF ALL ARMY TEAMS. WE HAVE STOPPED
> THE WAR TO CELEBRATE YOUR MAGNIFICENT SUCCESS.
>   MACARTHUR

The college game reaches a chaotic peak when a Poll Bowl presents itself to the nation.

A Poll Bowl is a game usually played late in the regular season, a game that will determine who is No. 1. These games are either called the Game of the Year, the Game of the Decade, or, if newspapers fall for it, the Game of the Century.

Old grads and school colors and geographic passions come out at Poll Bowls as at no other time. It is a game after which the winners will have bragging rights forever, and the losers will have to bury their sorrows until some future success erases—almost, but never quite—the awful memory of that tragic loss.

I am, admittedly, a Poll Bowl collector. I even collect the ones I never saw. Michigan–Minnesota in '40, for instance. Tom Harmon against Bruce Smith. Or Notre Dame–Army in '46. Johnny Lujack against Davis and Blanchard. I've covered every type of sporting classic in the past thirty-five years, but I am here to tell you that for pre-event excitement and suspense, for during-the-event drama, and for postevent deliberations, nothing in sport that I know of can come close to equaling a Poll Bowl.

I was lucky. I was privileged to cover the four most historical Poll Bowls of the past quarter century. They were all squeezed into a six-year period, from 1966 through 1971.

First came the 10–10 tie between Notre Dame and Michigan State at East Lansing in '66. What I remember best are the before and after. The game itself was error-filled. Before the game, Michigan State Coach Duffy Daugherty put Poll Bowls in perspective for an eternity when he said, "The game's not a matter of life and death. It's more important than that."

In the aftermath, I was flattered to learn that several Notre Dame students, encouraged by a wire service photographer, had set fire to a large pile of *Sports Illustrated* magazines containing my story of the game. In the story, I had hinted rather strongly that the Irish had tied one for the Gipper. The reason I wrote this was because Notre Dame Coach Ara Parseghian, whose team went into the game as No. 1, had run out the clock on the last series of downs, obviously willing to settle for a tie and trust in Notre Dame's power at the polls.

That story happened to inspire what was regarded at the time as a record amount of hate mail at *Sports Illustrated*, which taught me a lesson in journalism. If you're seriously into hate mail, all you have to do to get some is print the score of a game Notre Dame loses or ties.

I don't hate Notre Dame, by the way. I love Notre Dame, in fact, because I love college football, and college football wouldn't be the same without Notre Dame. How can anybody hate a university that has added so many refinements to nationwide recruiting, or, more importantly, done so much for the writers? Notre Dame invented the parking pass, the flip card, and the press box hotdog.

Notre Dame also has the best fight song and will hold the honor until Dixieland music makes a comeback and people rediscover the *Washington & Lee Swing.*

Anyhow, some of my best friends went to Notre Dame, just as some of my best friends are

Texas Aggies, whom I also don't hate. Texas A&M has the finest marching band in the civilized world—and the third-best fight song.

So onward.

When USC met UCLA before 90,000 in the Los Angeles Memorial Coliseum in 1967, there were only these incidental things at stake: the national title, the Pacific Coast championship, the Rose Bowl invitation, and the Heisman Trophy for either Gary Beban or O. J. Simpson.

It was a truly remarkable game in which Beban and Simpson outdid themselves. Beban passed for more than 300 yards, gave his team a 7–0 lead in the first quarter, a 14–14 tie in the third, and a 20–14 lead in the fourth. Simpson, who would win the Heisman a year after Beban, rushed for 177 yards. O. J. gave his team a 14–7 lead in the second quarter, and then a 21–20 victory in the fourth with an incredible touchdown run of 64 yards.

Later, in the Trojans' dressing room, a friend of John McKay's—me—found the USC coach in a cubicle, puffing on a victory cigar.

"What a game, John," I said, still excited. "It was a great win, but, my God, your heart has to go out to UCLA, doesn't it? They kept coming back. They could have beaten any other team in the country today."

John McKay, a man who would guide the Trojans to four national championships, was no UCLA lover—even though as a coach he could well understand the depth of pain that any rival would feel after the devastating, last-minute loss of a game so big. But UCLA was UCLA, the bitter crosstown enemy. McKay had to play the Bruins every season, and recruit against them all year long. So in that moment, when I was so eager to give the heartsick Bruins all of the credit they deserved for a heroic effort, McKay only looked up with a cynical grin, and said, "I've checked my heart. I don't have one."

In early December of 1969 Darrell Royal's Texas Longhorns went to Fayetteville, Arkansas, for their last game of the regular season, a holy war against the Arkansas Razorbacks. This was a Poll Bowl that the region and most of the country had been looking forward to since October. Texas and Arkansas were undefeated and untied, having each trampled ten opponents, and were nationally rated No. 1 (Texas) and No. 2 (Arkansas).

Since that particular season marked the centennial of college football, the game took on an added significance, so much so, in fact, that President Richard Nixon decided to fly in by helicopter on Saturday and present the winning coach, either Royal or Frank Broyles, with a special national championship plaque.

Tickets to the game were unavailable at any price, and the fans of both states went cuckoo. Ministers in both states actually asked for the Lord's help in obtaining victory.

In Fayetteville on Friday after the Longhorns had taken their final workout, Darrell Royal began putting on his "game face."

"Screw Arkansas," he said as we strolled across an exceptionally pretty part of the campus. "They put a pig on their head on Saturday, but all they do the rest of the week is sell jelly and cider by the side of the road."

That wasn't all that the Razorbacks did in the game. They almost ran Texas out of the stadium, taking a 14–0 lead into the fourth quarter. This was particularly shocking since Texas was a solid favorite and had looked unbeatable on paper. Unbeatable hadn't taken into consideration the four fumbles and two interceptions the Longhorns would lose.

The fourth quarter belonged to a little Texas quarterback named James Street, however. He wasn't fast but nobody caught him on a stunning, 42-yard touchdown run that put Texas back in the game, especially after he knifed across on a 2-point conversion play that narrowed the score to 14–8.

Street couldn't throw, either, but with only three minutes left, he hurled a 44-yard pass on fourth down, a daring gamble, to Randy Peschel, his tight end, and the play swept Texas to a 15–

14 victory and the second of Royal's three national championships as coach of the Longhorns.

Darrell Royal had "sucked it up" and called that brazen pass play, but it was later discovered that when Street relayed the call to the Texas huddle, Bob McKay, a Longhorn tackle, looked at the quarterback with a peculiar squint, and said, "Damn, James, you can't throw it that far!"

The moment I best recall on that trip to the Ozarks came in the press box. Jones Ramsey, then the director of sports information at the University of Texas, had been a tortured man throughout the afternoon, pacing, cursing, slowly resigning himself to a crushing defeat.

Now I was standing next to him as the clock ticked off the final seconds.

"Shit, I'd given up, " said Jones, " but thank God, James Street hadn't."

On Thanksgiving Day of 1971 in Norman, Oklahoma, the Nebraska Cornhuskers edged out the Oklahoma Sooners 35–31 in as thrilling a game as any No. 1 ever played against a No. 2. I don't believe any two powerhouse teams ever responded to the pressure and challenge of a Poll Bowl so well, or ever filled a stadium with so much superlative football for a full sixty minutes.

When Nebraska's Johnny Rodgers, Jeff Kinney, and Jerry Tagge would put the Cornhuskers ahead by as much as 14–3 and 28–17, Oklahoma's Jack Mildren, Greg Pruitt, and Jon Harrison would bring the Sooners back to lead by 17–14 and then by 31–28 through the middle of the final period.

Nebraska had another hero that day, a defensive nose guard named Rich Glover. Glover was everywhere, unblockable. He must have made seventy-five percent of the tackles, or so it seemed, and not only to me but to Nebraska coach Bob Devaney.

Devaney was a calm man on the surface, never one to show much emotion, and certainly never in public, never on the sideline. But there came a moment in the early part of the fourth quarter when I noticed Devaney hollering and gesturing to his players on the sideline. He was waving his arms and plainly looked angry. Not himself.

After the game, after Rodgers and Kinney and Tagge had ground out a winning drive of 80 yards, I asked Bob what he had been so exercised about earlier.

"You saw that, huh?"

"Yeah. On the sideline."

Devaney smiled and said, "Aw, I was just asking the kids if we had anybody who wanted to go in there and help Glover win the damn football game."

I confess to pronouncing the 1971 Nebraska–Oklahoma spectacle the greatest college game ever played—under the circumstances. I said this with my very own typewriter in *Sports Illustrated*'s very own magazine.

By comparison, the other Poll Bowls didn't quite measure up for one reason or another. In the '66 game between Notre Dame and Michigan State, neither team played very well, partly due to injuries. Texas, to be honest, played nervously and sloppily against Arkansas, or the "Nixon game" in 1969 would have had no suspense. And a haunting fact about the '67 USC–UCLA contest is that the Trojans benefited early—and were literally kept alive—by an interception for a cheap touchdown. There were no mistakes and no questionable performances in the Nebraska–Oklahoma game. Just a bunch of heroes living up to their press clippings.

Memories may not be the best thing about college football, but they are surely part of the charm.

And while I'm dealing with memories, I find myself tempted in this moment to put that USC–UCLA game of 1967 on a slightly higher pedestal for a reason that has nothing to do with Xs and Os. It was on that Saturday in the Los Angeles Coliseum, after all, that the Southern Cal students in the card section wittily spelled out "F. U. C. L. A."

Which, among other things, made it the Saturday that college football raised obscenity to an art form.

Kids

Opposite: In the autumn of 1974 I traveled across the country making photographs for a Sports Illustrated *picture essay on kids' football. The following images are drawn from that trek, a wonderful experience that brought my own boyhood back to me.*

Huddle. West Berlin, Vermont

Dreams. That's what putting on a uniform meant to me when I was his age. Wink, Texas

Above: "Come in a pound too heavy and you'll ride the bench." A tense moment for the young athlete who plays in a league organized by weight category. Los Angeles

Opposite: The most popular number in the 1970s was Joe Willie Namath's. Randalls Island, New York

Following pages: At a grammar school in Taos, New Mexico, I asked the principal if I could photograph some students after school. They ran one play for ten minutes—what we used to call "crazy" football.

Most kids enjoy being photographed: one cheerleader scowled at me all day while her friends giggled. Los Angeles

Pop Warner League. A spearing injury. Los Angeles

Players listening to a pregame talk by the coach. Randalls Island, New York

A one-room schoolhouse during the peak week for autumn leaves—and scrimmages. This is as pure and sweet as sport can be. West Berlin, Vermont

The face of this child and the compassion of his coach make this photograph a favorite of mine.
Barre, Vermont

Above: I've always thought of this lad as a little O. J. He's got the form, the style, the equipment, even the star on the helmet. Los Angeles

Following pages: I went out one morning in New York to take some shots of the city in autumn fog. As I passed through the Sheep Meadow in Central Park I saw a team practicing.

Backyard football. Barre, Vermont

Above: A boy and his football are seldom parted. West Berlin, Vermont

Following page: Anyplace you can find a flat surface you've got a playing field. Pella, Iowa

The College Game

The Turf

On September 14, 1968, in Knoxville, Tennessee, when Walter Iooss's cameras and my typewriter covered the first game played on artificial turf, I honestly didn't think of it as the day that would change football forever. Neither did Walter. We didn't know then that the synthetic surface would become so popular, the whole damn sport would get carpeted.

Frankly, all I thought after the Saturday afternoon on that rim of the Smokies was that I had witnessed a rather exceptionally exciting opening day of college football. The Tennessee Volunteers had fought back to tie the Georgia Bulldogs, 17–17, with no time left on the clock.

As for the artificial turf, I *did* point out in my story that it was still as rich green and spotless after the game as it had been before a truckload of Tennessee cheerleaders had driven on it, before a Tennessee walking horse had pranced around on it, before a Georgia bulldog had gnawed at it, before a Georgia coach had flicked ashes on it, and before a black kid had played on it—which hadn't happened every day in the Southeastern Conference.

"The verdict has to be that artificial turf is okay," I wrote, straining for a gag. "God blew it when he gave us grass."

That was the view from the press box. Down on the field, Walter had a different experience.

This was the sixties, mind you, and in keeping with the fashion of those days, Walter's hair looked like Prince Valiant had collided with a damp mop. In the South, they weren't quite ready for the way Walter looked.

Early in the second quarter, after he'd rushed around the stadium floor seeking camera angles, Walter found himself standing next to a uniformed policeman on the sideline. The belly. The drawl. You know the guy.

"Your foot touched that line, boy," the officer said. Remember the Dodge commercial? Walter thought he was in one.

"What?" said Walter, startled.

"Your foot touched that sideline."

"I'm shooting for *Sports Illustrated*," Walter said, thinking that if he dropped the name of his calling card, the officer would be impressed.

"Your foot's been touchin' that line all day," the officer said.

"I'll be careful," Walter said, fondling the cameras draped around his neck and shoulders.

"I'm gonna be watchin' your foot, boy."

"Yes, sir."

"See these notches, boy?"

The officer showed Walter his night stick. It had several notches in it.

"That's nice," said Walter.

"Know what them notches is for?"

"No, sir."

"Them notches is for hippies."

"Really?"

"Ever time I hit me a hippie, I put a notch in my stick."

"I can see that."

"You want to be one of them notches, boy?"

"No, sir, I sure don't," Walter said.

"You watch your foot, then. Don't put your foot on that line. You put your foot on that line again, boy, you gonna be a notch."

Walter didn't become a notch, happily, but he did spend the rest of the day shooting with a long lens.

Opposite: Stopping at a highway grocery to get something to drink after a University of Texas game, I spotted this Longhorn fan in the parking lot. October 1977. Somewhere in Texas

This shot was taken during the first college game played on artificial turf. A sad Saturday for football traditionalists. September 1968. Neyland Stadium, Knoxville, Tennessee

Following pages:
Left: A shoulder separation: I've always felt uncomfortable photographing these situations.
University of Oklahoma vs. Miami of Ohio. October 1973. Owen Field, Norman, Oklahoma

Right: A Los Angeles character called Gypsy Boots (right), who used to appear on the Steve Allen
Show, was a dedicated USC fan. November 1976. Los Angeles Memorial Coliseum

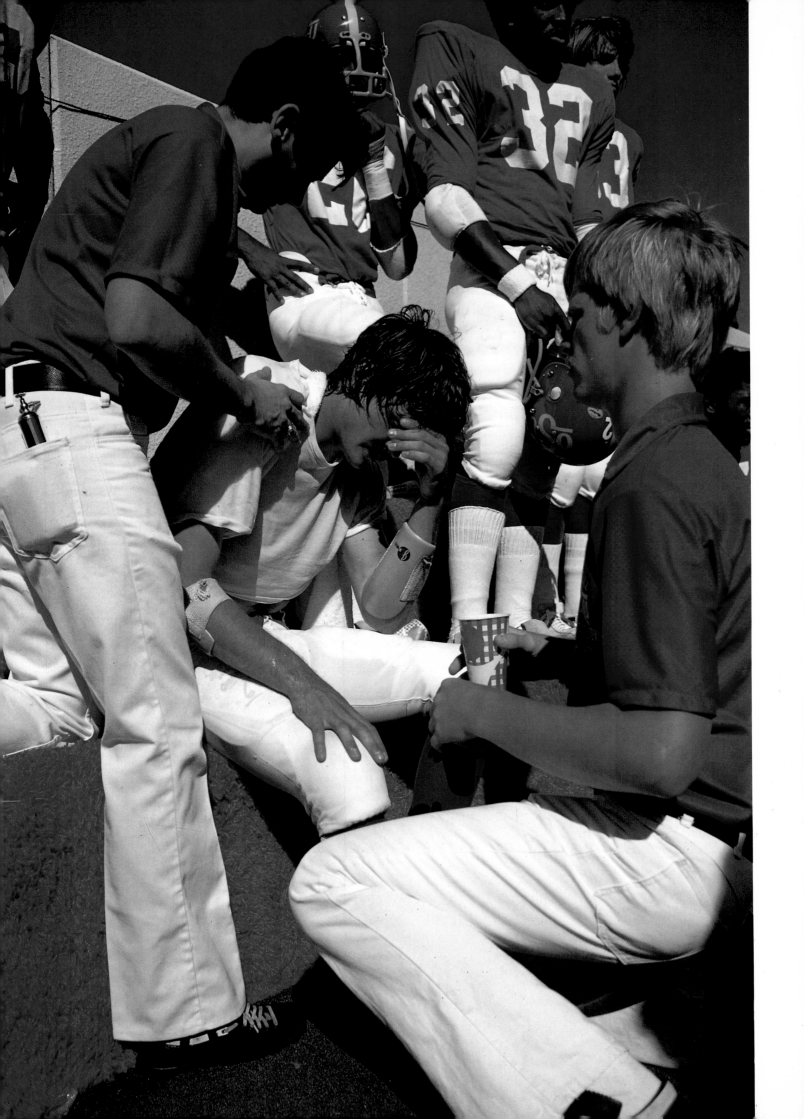

Opposite: When I made this picture in 1965, I was only a few years older than these players. Spartan Stadium, East Lansing, Michigan

Above: Ricky Bell, twice a runner-up for the Heisman Trophy, waiting for a postgame interview after a USC–UCLA game. Ricky passed away in November of 1984 while still playing for Tampa Bay. November 1976. Los Angeles Memorial Coliseum

Throughout this USC–UCLA game I used a 1,000mm lens to get the red and blue staircase of the coliseum in the background with a player in the foreground. November 1976. Los Angeles Memorial Coliseum

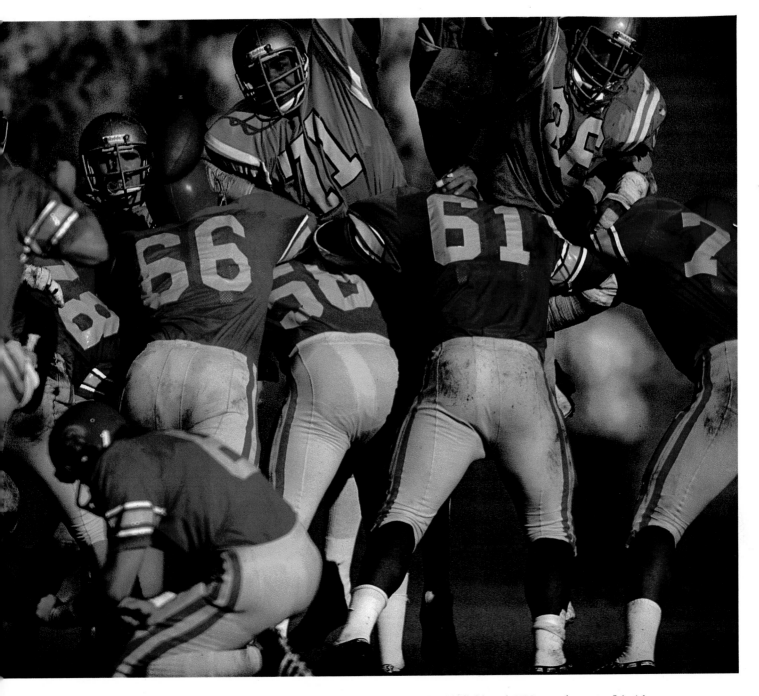

Above: With the same long lens, at the same game, I caught this field goal. USC won the game, 24–14.

Following pages:
Left: On assignment to photograph the high-stepping Grambling State University marching band, I saw this drum major, his shadow, another drum major's shadow, and my shadow late one afternoon at a rehearsal at Yankee Stadium in the Bronx.

Right: This picture remains as vivid to me as if I took it yesterday. George Webster (90) celebrates the sacking of the Ohio State quarterback for a safety. 1965. Spartan Stadium

*Texas Tech quarterback Tom Wilson (13). I've never seen a delivery like this. c. 1965. Jones Stadium,
Lubbock, Texas*

A Gator Bowl celebration. I always wished the cheerleaders would hug me at the game's end.
Jacksonville, Florida

The Bear

Paul (Bear) Bryant was an overwhelming presence. Because of his physical size, his winning reputation, and a look in his eyes that always suggested he knew more than he was willing to say, it was generally felt both by those who knew him well and those who only admired him from afar that he was the real John Wayne. It wouldn't have surprised any of Bryant's scores of worshippers, a number that included myself, to hear that he had walked into the middle of a riot, or an unruly demonstration, or even a minor war, and put an end to it simply by looking mildly displeased, and perhaps saying, "What the hell's going on here? You people get on home now."

Bryant never saw his mystique put to a test that severe. Known as Bear to his fans and the public and Paul to his friends, he used it all up on football. And in this regard, the main thing to be said about him is that he was, beyond any argument or doubt, the greatest football coach who ever lived.

Proof?

Well, aside from the fact that Bryant finally won more games than Amos Alonzo Stagg or any other major college coach in history, he was the man who taught all of his contemporaries and many of today's geniuses most of what they know about how to recruit, how to motivate athletes, how to organize a staff, how to delegate authority, how to run a game from the sideline, how to improvise on offense and defense, how to prepare for a big one, how to grade game films, how to deal with success, how to handle the alumni, and how to romance the press.

While Bryant knew he was good at all of the above, he liked to credit his athletes for most of the fame he achieved. He preferred kids who had dedication over those with size or speed, kids who came from "good Mommas and Poppas." And these were the types with whom he won most of his games.

The ultimate proof of Bryant's coaching brilliance makes itself obvious in the chart I've prepared that's lodged further down in these paragraphs. But before you get there, I have some stories that say a good bit about the man's awesome mystique.

Some of his close friends like to tell about the time in Tuscaloosa when Bryant was forced to deal with what could only be called an "ethnic problem."

You may recall that it was during the mid-seventies when many black players around the country were starting to wear headbands. At Alabama, the subject hadn't come up, but it was pretty much assumed by Bryant's players that the coach had a rule against any player wearing a headband.

Bear Bryant. Auburn at Alabama. November 29, 1974. Bryant-Denny Stadium, Tuscaloosa, Alabama

Eventually, however, Bryant was confronted in his office one day by a committee of three players who had come forward to ask if the team's best running back, a black kid, could be allowed to wear a headband.

One of the players said, "He thinks it'll give him pride, Coach. It's part of his heritage."

Bryant stared coldly at the players, then said, "I have no problem with that."

The visitors were, of course, stunned. They were relieved, but nevertheless stunned.

They thanked the coach in a mixed chorus of voices, smiled feebly, and began shuffling toward the door to leave.

Bryant returned to some paperwork on his desk, but added in a voice they could hear:

"He can wear his headband . . . or his helmet."

For all of his national championship seasons, there was still the one that got away. The season was 1966, Ken Stabler's junior year, when the Crimson Tide wound up with the only perfect record in the land and yet lost out in the polls to the once-tied but ever-popular Notre Dame.

The '66 team was a typically small Alabama outfit, but it may have been Bryant's quickest, proudest, and most efficient team. Stabler was the best combination of passer, runner, and leader that Bryant ever had at quarterback, and Stabler's passing was aided by the fact that he had two absolutely great receivers in Ray Perkins and Dennis Homan. Alabama defeated eleven opponents that season, and ten of them didn't come within shouting distance of the Tide. Ah, but the other one.

In the middle of October, Alabama had to invade Tennessee, never a pleasant task, for as Bryant often said, "They play too much like we do." To make matters worse, this was a bunch of quick-hitting Volunteers who had lost only one game the previous season.

On that rainy, dreary Saturday, Tennessee "took it to 'em," as they say. The Volunteers led by 10–0 at the half. But in the dressing room, Bryant said, "That was their half. This one's ours."

Slowly and grudgingly, then, Stabler's running and passing produced a touchdown and a 2-point conversion, narrowing the score to 10–8, but with five minutes to play, the Tide still trailed, and Alabama was 75 yards away from the Tennessee goal. And it was raining.

No matter. Stabler put together a heartstopping drive that carried the Tide to within a few feet of the Tennessee end zone. Steve Davis was then called upon to kick a field goal. It was good. Alabama went ahead by the odd score of 11–10, but the game wasn't over. With less than three minutes to go, Tennessee roared back with a desperate drive of its own. The Vols whirled 71 yards to the Alabama 2-yard line where, with only sixteen seconds remaining, they set up for a field goal from a slight angle. The snap was good, the hold was good, but the kick was wide by a hair. Alabama had survived.

Later in the locker room, Bryant went on at length about his team's winning drive, how his players had refused to quit, how this was a team that would always find a way to win because it totally rejected the idea of losing.

Finally, a writer broke in, and said, "Coach, aren't you overlooking something? What would you have done there at the end if that Tennessee kid had kicked the ball *straight?*"

With a stern look and without hesitating, Bryant said, "Blocked it."

As a journalist, I particularly enjoyed Bryant's efforts at show biz.

Sitting in his office one day in the early sixties, I listened patiently as he talked about the kind of dedication a kid needed to be a winner. He loved a hitter more than anything.

An Alabama helmet—crimson with a white stripe from front to back—rested on a table by Bryant's desk.

"See that helmet," he nodded. "That belonged to a hitter, Lee Roy Jordan. Look at it close. It's got the colors of every team we played on it."

I examined the helmet, noticing the tiny smudges of Auburn blue, Georgia Tech gold, LSU purple, Tennessee orange, Mississippi State maroon, and so on.

Very impressive, except that I wasn't a cub reporter. I'd been around football long enough to know that most teams cleaned and polished their helmets before every game.

"Who's your artist?" I grinned.

"Damn sportswriters," Bryant said with a shrug. "It works like hell on recruits, though."

About this chart. The first national poll was instituted in 1924. In the more than sixty years since then, as the number of legitimate polls and selectors has certainly increased (AP, UPI, Football Writers, Hall of Fame, et cetera), it remains that only twenty coaches—and an equally exclusive sixteen schools—have been able to win the mythical national championship more than once. Like they say. Once can be luck, but twice means talent. In what follows, Bryant's name sits atop a rather fierce list of coaching immortals:

Coach, School	National Titles	Years Won
Bear Bryant, Alabama	6	1961, 1964, 1965, 1973, 1978, 1979
Frank Leahy, Notre Dame	5	1943, 1946, 1947, 1949, 1953
Howard Jones, Southern Cal	5	1928, 1931, 1932, 1933, 1939
John McKay, Southern Cal	4	1962, 1967, 1972, 1974
Woody Hayes, Ohio State	4	1954, 1957, 1961, 1968
Bernie Bierman, Minnesota	4	1934, 1936, 1940, 1941
Knute Rockne, Notre Dame	3	1924, 1929, 1930
Darrell Royal, Texas	3	1963, 1969, 1970
Barry Switzer, Oklahoma	3	1974, 1975, 1985
Ara Parseghian, Notre Dame	3	1964, 1966, 1973
Bud Wilkinson, Oklahoma	3	1950, 1955, 1956
Bob Neyland, Tennessee	3	1940, 1950, 1951
Dutch Meyer, TCU	2	1935, 1938
Red Blaik, Army	2	1944, 1945
Bob Devaney, Nebraska	2	1970, 1971
Wally Butts, Georgia	2	1942, 1946
Jim Tatum, Maryland	2	1951, 1953
Duffy Daugherty, Michigan State	2	1965, 1966
Johnny Vaught, Ole Miss	2	1960, 1962
Jock Sutherland, Pittsburgh	2	1936, 1937

Despite all of Bryant's successes, there were two things he never did. In three games against each, he never beat Notre Dame or Texas. This fact was never lost on his loyal followers, and it leads to a concluding anecdote.

A few years ago, I ran into an attractive, middle-aged lady with a Southern accent at a cocktail party in Fort Worth. She introduced herself to me, saying she had read some of my stuff. She and her husband lived in Texas now, she said, but they were *from* Alabama and were two of Bryant's staunchest advocates.

Because I had written so much about college football, the lady obviously knew I would understand it when she said, in the course of the conversation, "We're happy here, but there are three things I want to do before I die. I want to see Alabama beat Notre Dame. I want to see Alabama beat Texas. And I want to go to Europe."

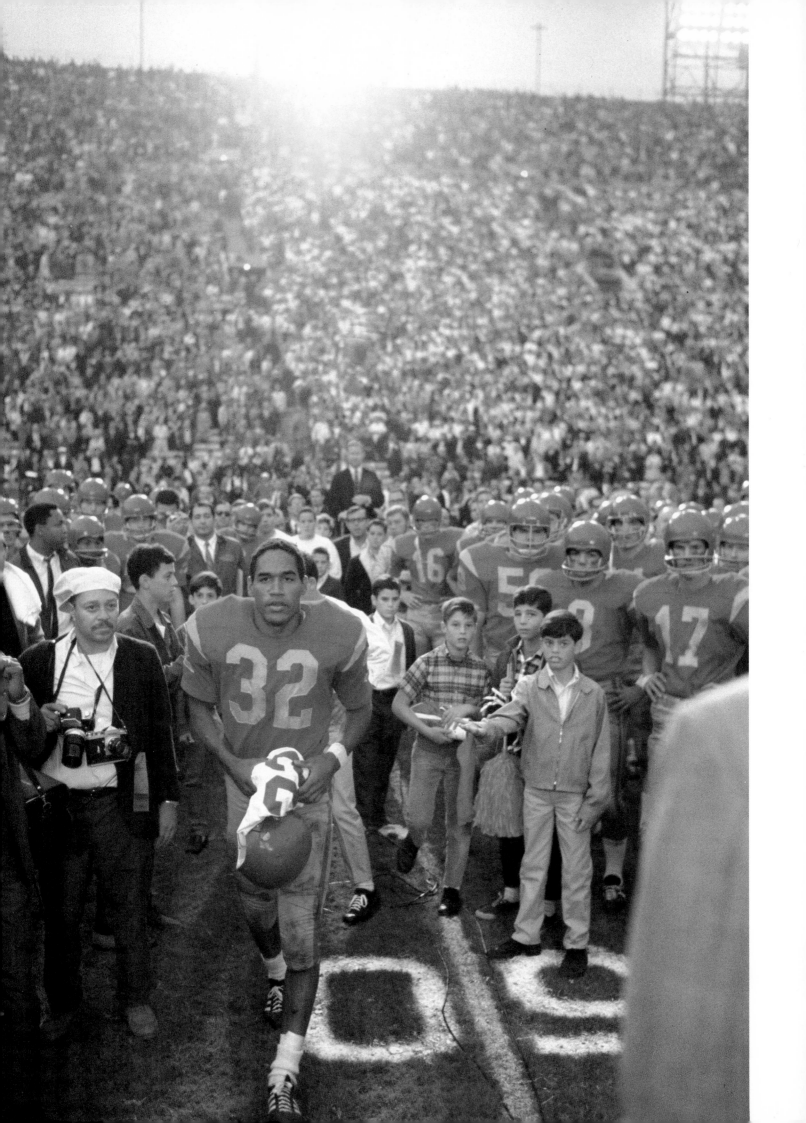

The Juice

Arguments have always raged over who was football's greatest running back, and the usual suspects are always rounded up: Red Grange, Tom Harmon, Ernie Nevers, Doak Walker, Jim Brown. For myself and many others, the dispute ended with O. J. Simpson.

At 6′ 2″ and 207 pounds, and with the authentic speed of 9.4 in the 100-yard dash, no player ever carried a football with such combined power and speed—and moves—as O. J. Case closed. I have spoke.

Orenthal James Simpson—O. J., Orange Juice, The Juice—came out of the Potrero Hill ghetto of San Francisco and ran to glory first at the University of Southern California and then with the Buffalo Bills in the NFL.

In his two seasons at USC, against the toughest college teams in America, he ran for an astonishing 3,124 yards. He led the Trojans to the national championship in 1967 and captured the Heisman Trophy for himself in 1968. Five years later at Buffalo, on a team without much help, he spent a single season rushing for 2,003 yards, becoming the first NFL back to topple the magic 2,000-yard barrier.

It was back in those college stadiums, however, that O. J. left his most vivid impressions. With his long, piercing stride and his bruising power at breaking tackles, he was virtually unstoppable. Sooner or later, he would break one. And when he did, he was uncatchable.

In the season of '67, USC coach John McKay took his Trojans to South Bend, Indiana, to meet a Notre Dame Squad that was rated No. 1 at the time, the defending national champion, in fact, from most of the polls the previous year.

O. J. left the Irish strewn all over the field that day, carrying the Trojans to a 24–7 victory.

When sportswriters later asked John McKay why he called on his tailback to carry the ball so often, McKay said, "I'll tell him when he's tired. He's not in a union."

That same afternoon, after O. J. had reeled off another startling, broken-field run, Notre Dame's publicity man, Roger Valdiseri, turned to me, and said:

"O. J. doesn't stand for Orange Juice. It stands for, 'Oh, Jesus, there he goes again!' "

O. J's college career left such a burning impression on everyone that in 1969 when the sport celebrated its centennial, a nationwide poll of football writers was taken to name the All-Time Team.

In the backfield after 100 years were Sam Baugh, Red Grange, Doak Walker—and O. J. Simpson, who had only been out of college a year!

An amusing fact in Simpson's past is that he had once tried to play organized kiddie football as a twelve-year-old, but he never got the chance. In San Francisco, the coach had told him he wasn't good enough, to run along home.

He ran to the Hall of Fame instead.

Opposite: O. J. Simpson hasn't changed much since his college days. This picture was taken at his last game for USC at the coliseum. In that game, Notre Dame tied USC. November 1968. Los Angeles Memorial Coliseum

The Pros

Now and then I like to remind people that pro football was a blue collar sport for fifty years, a game mostly played by fat guys in the baseball parks of industrial cities. It didn't become chic until television.

This doesn't mean the pro game lacks charm altogether or hasn't provided us with many a nervous thrill. It simply means in my own mind that the professional game will never seem as important, as necessary, if you will, as college football. But this is my own problem, not yours, and Walter Iooss's photographs indicate that it has never been his.

The odd thing today is that pro football is becoming too corporate, and this in turn forces me to be more intrigued with its past. I don't suppose that's surprising. I've always suffered attacks of nostalgia for things I never knew. These days, in any event, the more I try to watch a game that is played indoors on carpet with the memory bank of a computer telling a coach whether he wants to run or pass, the more I miss Jim Thorpe and the Canton Bulldogs.

That's an exaggeration. I don't miss Jim Thorpe and the Canton Bulldogs as much as I miss Red Grange and Bronko Nagurski, or Sam Baugh (of course) and Don Hutson, or Bobby Layne and Doak Walker, or Sonny Jurgensen and Frank Gifford, or Don Meredith and Jake Scott—just to get a maniacal defender in there—or even Terry Bradshaw. Bradshaw's awfully recent but he was a rough-edged throwback to the thirties, a guy whose competitive instincts and reckless heroics somehow managed to defy the computer printouts.

Bradshaw led the Pittsburgh Steelers to four Super Bowl victories in the 1970s, basically by taking off on a busted play at some given moment and throwing the football into the fading twilight and finding out later, after getting knocked on his butt, that Lynn Swann or John Stallworth had leaped about thirty feet in the air and come down with the pass.

There was something wonderfully noncorporate about the way Bradshaw and the Steelers dominated the sport during those years. They were especially appealing to those of us who knew where pro football had come from.

For the most part, it came from factory workers.

In the beginning, there was rarely ever any talk about upside potential or downside risks when a man hired a bunch of meat packers to go out and play a bunch of guys from the brewery, the mill, or the mines.

It gave the guys a diversion, anyhow. They were hulkish sportsmen who weren't nimble enough to make it in baseball, the only professional sport that paid a living wage. In the factories, the hours were long and exhausting and the take-home pay small, so why not release your frustrations in a game of football?

Today when a TV network collects a million dollars for a one-minute commercial on a Super Bowl telecast, the executives in charge ought to drink a toast to a man named George Halas instead of themselves.

Halas was a salesman for a starch company in Decatur, Illinois, when he first began trying to organize pro football, to make it a business.

Halas eventually organized the league, and reorganized it more than once, but he never lured many followers until his Decatur Staleys (the starch company) became the Chicago Bears and he signed a player named Harold (Red) Grange out of the University of Illinois. Red Grange, Old 77, the Galloping Ghost, the Wheaton Iceman—he must still hold the nickname record—had already become a national treasure. In a game against Michigan, he had electrified the world with dizzying touchdown runs of 95, 67, 54, and 44 yards.

Grange's first appearances as a pro were more like happenings, concerts, than football games. More than 36,000 went to see him at Wrigley Field his first time out. Two weeks later, over 66,000 poured into the Polo Grounds in New York to watch his ghostlike gallops. Pro football had a chance.

It didn't have the league as we know it until 1933. And it didn't have the forward pass as we know it until TCU's Sam Baugh went to the Washington Redskins in 1937 and quickly convinced the pros that the pass was a weapon to be used on any play, from anywhere on the field. Baugh passed the Redskins to the NFL championship in his rookie season, and no rookie quarterback has done it since.

Largely because of Baugh, college football had already realized the forward pass was an offensive staple. Sam had thrown on just about every other down in 1935 when he pitched TCU to the national title and then a Sugar Bowl victory. With a weaker team in '36, he had thrown even more as he became a two-time All-American, but TCU had to settle for a win over Marquette in the inaugural Cotton Bowl.

Sam was more than a passer; far more. He was also the best punter anybody ever saw, and he generally led the Redskins in interceptions. Uh-huh. They played both ways then. Those were the days. Sixty-minute men like Baugh, no face masks, muddy fields, wet footballs, long train rides, no business managers, very few stock options.

After the Slinger had become a contented rancher in West Texas, I had an occasion to ask him about the hardship days of pro football.

"We thought it beat workin'," is essentially what he said about it.

I like to think of a player like Sam Baugh today every time I read about a guy on some specialty team who's having a labor dispute with his club management.

It is impossible to say that any one thing sent the NFL into the stratosphere of high finance. Certainly it was love at first sight for TV and pro football, but other sports have failed on television, or failed to prosper as pro football has. I believe it has something to do with the basic appeal of the game itself. Football is the closest we can come to the Christians and the lions without actually getting anybody killed. Then, too, the pros get a lot of carry-over value from the college game. And finally, they've benefited from some rather decent drama of their own making.

It's entirely possible that the championship game played on Sunday, December 28, 1958, in Yankee Stadium had more to do with pro football becoming fashionable than anything before or since. That game between the Baltimore Colts and New York Giants was, granted, outrageously exciting, one that mesmerized a national TV audience, but I don't agree that it was "the greatest football game ever played," as so many historians have called it. Just because America heard three words for the first time—sudden death overtime—doesn't make the game *that* good.

On the contrary, I like to argue that if Frank Gifford, my friend and hero, suffers the loss of three fumbles, which he did, the game can't possibly be called great, or even a bed of roses. I was rooting for the Giants, you see. For Gifford, Kyle Rote, Charley Conerly, Pat Summerall, and all those guys I thought were representing Toots Shor's, "21," and Big Apple glamour.

The game did have a few things going for it, even before it got to sudden death. Long runs. Long passes. Rapid, swirling action. With two minutes to play in regulation, the Giants led, 17–14. But the Colts had Johnny Unitas and friends.

Unitas passed the Colts to a tying field goal by Steve Myhra with twelve seconds left on the clock in cold, blustery, and nerve-racked Yankee Stadium. Then came the luckiest commercial spot in history. And then people called their friends everywhere to turn on the TV and watch this thing called sudden death.

In the overtime, the Giants had the ball first but couldn't move it, so here came Unitas again, hitting Raymond Berry and Lenny Moore and Jim Mutscheller in the weary Giant secondary. Unitas drove the Colts to New York's 10-yard line, which was where something mysterious happened, something that's baffled football minds ever since.

Instead of winning the game with a field goal right there, Unitas risked a pass out in the flat to Mutscheller. He made a tumbling catch at the one. And then Alan Ameche barged in for the touchdown that made the final score Baltimore 23, Giants 17.

To this day, there are grown men who believe that Unitas—and Baltimore coach Weeb Ewbank—were either confused or in shock and thought you had to score a *touchdown* to win in overtime. And there are other grown men who think the Colts needed that touchdown to "cover the points." And there are still other grown men who think Unitas was "dumb," to be blunt about it, by risking an interception on the flat pass to Mutscheller and then risking a fumble on Ameche's blast through right tackle instead of ending it with a field goal.

Unitas has been asked about his play selections a million times since that Sunday, and he's never told me anything he hasn't told anyone else.

"I took what they gave me," he's said. "Besides, I never expected interceptions when I threw the ball."

In sports, nothing breeds glamour like winning. I haven't seen that statement carved into too much granite, but it has to be the only explanation for the popularity of the Green Bay Packers—Vince Lombardi's Packers—in the 1960s. Boy, were they dull. And yet the cult of NFL fanatics kept increasing.

Maybe it's because the Packers were among the few things around in those days that were reliable. You couldn't believe in governments, or wars, or the youth, but you could believe in the Packers.

Lombardi's Packers were a good old American work-ethic football team. Forrest Gregg, Jerry Kramer, and Fuzzy Thurston would knock people down. Jim Taylor and Paul Hornung would run to daylight. Occasionally, the unspectacular but efficient Bart Starr would throw a pass to somebody like Boyd Dowler, who would be open by 40 yards because the opponents would be preoccupied with trying to keep the Packers from running to daylight.

Lombardi became such an example of leadership that corporate executives began stealing lines from him when they addressed their nail-biting MBAs. "You don't do things right once in a while. You do them right all the time!"

For my money, the best quote *about* Lombardi came from Henry Jordan, the defensive tackle who died of a heart attack at the far too early age of forty-two. Jordan was once asked to comment on Lombardi's code of fairness in dealing with his players. He said, "Vince treats all of us the same. Like dogs."

It didn't seem possible that any team could out-dull the Packers, and yet Don Shula's Miami Dolphins almost did in the early seventies. But they were winners and therefore they took on a glow.

Most of the excitement that Miami created happened in the offensive line where Bob Kuechenberg and Larry Little planted crops and harvested touchdowns. They made Larry Csonka look like a broken-field runner. Quarterback Bob Griese presided over the Dolphins in a workmanlike, Bart Starr sort of way. As a strategist, Shula embellished George Allen's Nickel Defense, which didn't overexcite as many opposing passers as it did TV announcers.

In 1973, the Dolphins did what they could to put the word "parity" in a coffin. They plodded to a perfect record of 17–0. After Miami had accomplished this with the Super Bowl victory over Washington, somebody asked Csonka if Shula might reward the Dolphins with something special in the way of cars or bonuses or what have you.

"He'll probably give us Monday off," said Csonka.

Then came the fun-loving Pittsburgh Steelers. The Steelers managed to be fun-loving *despite* Chuck Noll, a coach who kept wanting to be thought of as a "teacher" in the mold of Lombardi and Shula.

The Steelers made it seem just the opposite. It seemed that in their own way, they taught Chuck Noll how to win football games. They either did it with Terry Bradshaw's bombs to Swann and Stallworth, which were at least partly successful because of a ballcarrier named Franco Harris, or they did it with Jack Lambert and the Steel Curtain.

I think sportswriters should all be terribly grateful to these Steelers for one thing alone: they always made the Super Bowl interesting.

In fact, the Steelers were embroiled in the only Super Bowl game that has been suitable for framing. By that I mean the only one that was tightly contested all the way and worth remembering for its suspense and the football excellence of both teams.

This was the tenth Super Bowl, the one after the 1975 season, a game played in Miami's Orange Bowl on a gorgeous day. It was a bitter contest between the Steelers, who may have been at their peak, and for once, a *physical* Dallas Cowboys team that was also unpredictable. These were not just the Cowboys of Tom Landry's advanced math, they were the Cowboys of scrambling Roger Staubach and Drew Pearson's miracle catches, the Cowboys of Cliff Harris and Charlie Waters, of D. D. Lewis and a young Hollywood Henderson. They had the arm, the hands, and they had hitters.

It was a brutal game all the way, interspersed with big plays. Despite a psychotic performance by Pittsburgh's Jack Lambert at linebacker—"I hate the Cowboys," he'd said, "and if the sharks don't eat Staubach, I will."—Dallas took a 10–7 lead into the fourth quarter. Pittsburgh chipped away to make it 10–9, then to go ahead by 12–10, and then by 15–10. But strangely the momentum seemed to stay with Dallas, and you kept thinking that surely the next time the Cowboys get the ball . . .

That was until there were only three minutes left in the game and Bradshaw ordered a play called 69 Maximum Flanker Post. Terry must have thrown the ball 70 yards in the air. He was knocked cold by a blitzing Cliff Harris a split second after he unloaded it, so he never saw Lynn Swann's soaring catch for the touchdown that iced the game, enabling Pittsburgh to withstand a closing Dallas touchdown that made the final score read 21–17, Steelers.

Bradshaw did not know what he had wrought until the game was over. "I was in the locker room before I could kind of understand it," he said.

I've always thought it was fortunate for pro football that the Steelers and Cowboys had provided all of us sportswriters with so much entertainment in that Super Bowl. Throughout the long afternoon, Raquel Welch had been a visitor in the press box.

A confession. I've had trouble digesting those cerebral championships that were taken by Bill

Walsh's San Francisco 49ers. My own mind tends to reject the city of San Francisco ever winning anything other than the Nouvelle Cuisine Bowl. It should be said, however, that the 49ers' Joe Montana joined what may be the most elite club in the NFL with those triumphs. Only Sam Baugh (TCU and the Redskins), Joe Namath (Alabama and the Jets), and Joe Montana (Notre Dame and the 49ers) have ever quarterbacked teams that won both a national championship in college and a world championship in the pros.

It will be a while before we know whether Mike Ditka's Chicago Bears are going to be a dynasty on the order of Sid Luckman's Bears. But I don't think it's too early to acknowledge that the Bears' William (Refrigerator) Perry, ex-Clemson, magna cum lunchmeat, has already replaced John Madden as pro football's most popular Mondo Rotundo.

There is one last organization that deserves mention. It has never been a dynasty in the truest sense, but it has always been a presence, something that haunted the league like a dark tornado cloud. I speak of the Raiders. The ugly old black-and-silver Raiders of Oakland, Los Angeles, and Al Davis, but not of Commissioner Pete Rozelle. Pete is the most talented public relations man in the history of sporting executives, but he couldn't keep the Raiders in Oakland.

Like him or not and believe him or not, you can't take a lot of things away from Al Davis. He's a fighter. He's shrewd. He's manipulative. He's a con artist. He has a brilliant football mind. The ultimate proof comes in his three NFL championships, his three Super Bowl victories. Yeah, there've been all those street-smart, alley-cat headhunters who won the games for him, but Al *was* the Raiders, he *is* the Raiders.

Walter Iooss's last photograph in this book (page 176) says it all about Al Davis—and football. It's a closeup shot of Al Davis's hands. Here we can see Al's fingernails practically chewed to the bone. This sometimes goes with winning. And here we see his last Super Bowl ring, a ring that celebrates all three of the Raiders' championships.

Funny, huh? The manly game of football spends fifty years in a gouging, snarling heap. It spends another fifty years trying to refine and sharpen the violence. And after all of these bruising years and all of this violence, it winds up in the 1980s with a bunch of tough, beefy guys all chasing after a very curious thing.

Jewelry.

Opposite: I gave Lyle Alzado a simple request—look intense. July 1984. Los Angeles Raiders training camp, Santa Rosa, California

Following pages: I saw this orange wall of doors at Mile High Stadium and staked it out. A player I can't remember peered out for no more than five seconds and the photograph was made.

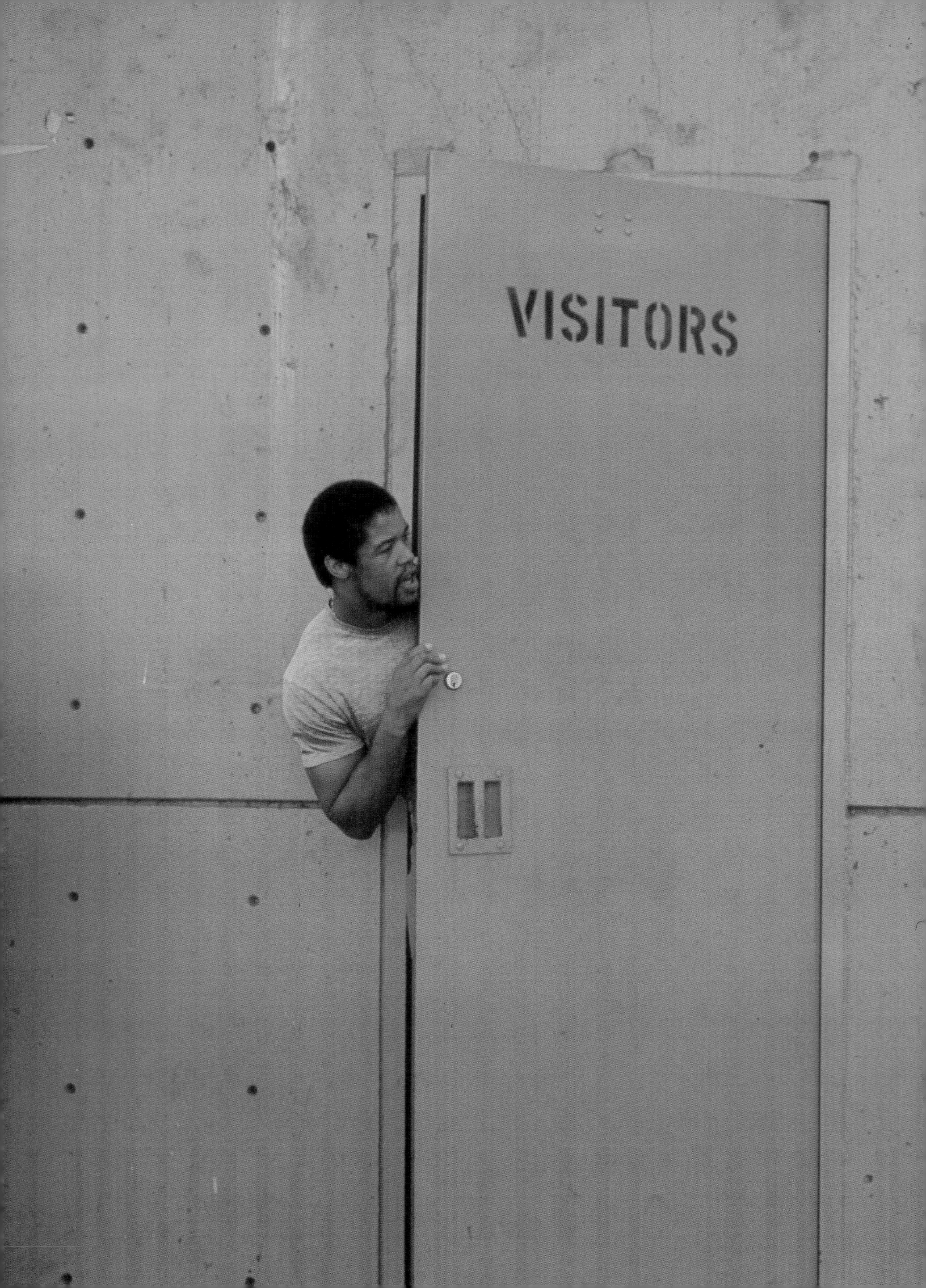
VISITORS

OFFICIALS

*Quarterbacks Earl Morrall and Johnny Unitas and defensive back Jerry Logan suit up in the Colts'
locker room. November 1968. Tiger Stadium, Detroit*

*Above and opposite: Some players are boisterous and talkative in the locker room, some go inward.
In these photographs, Billy Joe DuPree (above) and defensive end Harvey Martin (opposite) of the
Cowboys screen out distractions to get into their game mood. September 1981. Pontiac Silverdome,
Pontiac, Michigan*

A tunnel leads from the visitors' clubhouse in Cleveland to the field. I saw this scene once before and went back to catch Franco Harris for this shot. October 1979. Cleveland Stadium

Above: There was a strange, calm sense of solitude as Walter Payton and I were the only ones left in the tunnel, with 60,000 screaming fans just a few feet away. 1979. Veterans Stadium, Philadelphia

Following pages: This picture, my favorite of all shots of Texas Stadium, was made with a 17mm lens as Cowboys kicker Rafael Septien came on the field to begin the second half. December 1981. Texas Stadium, Irving, Texas

At the Steelers training camp in Latrobe, Pennsylvania, I spent four days trying to get Mean Joe Greene to look mean, but he was always smiling. The last day I was there I had Joe in a perfect setting for the shot, but he had a team meeting in five minutes and if he was late he would be fined. I stalled and Joe became angrier every second, until finally he glared at me, I snapped the shutter, and he said, "I'm splittin'." 1973

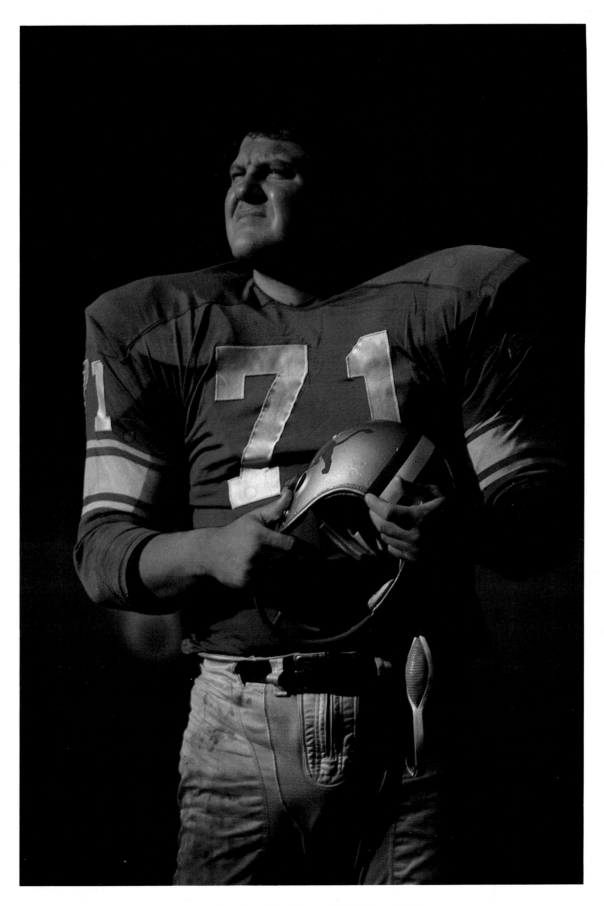

A cover for SI on Alex Karras. 1964. Tiger Stadium

These four pictures (and the one on page 116) were made during the 1985 season, when I covered the Dolphins on a special assignment for SI. Above: This cookie vendor at the Orange Bowl in Miami is known to one and all as Sabbires. September 1985. Below: Dan Marino relaxes in the canvas walkway leading from the locker room. October 20, 1985. Orange Bowl

Above: Short-yardage specialist Woody Bennett (34) leaves the field at halftime against New England in the rain. December 1985. Orange Bowl. Below: Left outside linebacker Bob Brudzinski takes a breather from weight training at the Dolphins practice field. December 1985. Orange Bowl

Above: Muscles are not everything: this rookie at training camp did not make the Los Angeles Raiders. July 1984. Los Angeles Raiders training camp

Opposite: The unknown Steeler: this rookie was cut after a preseason night game at Three Rivers Stadium in Pittsburgh. 1973

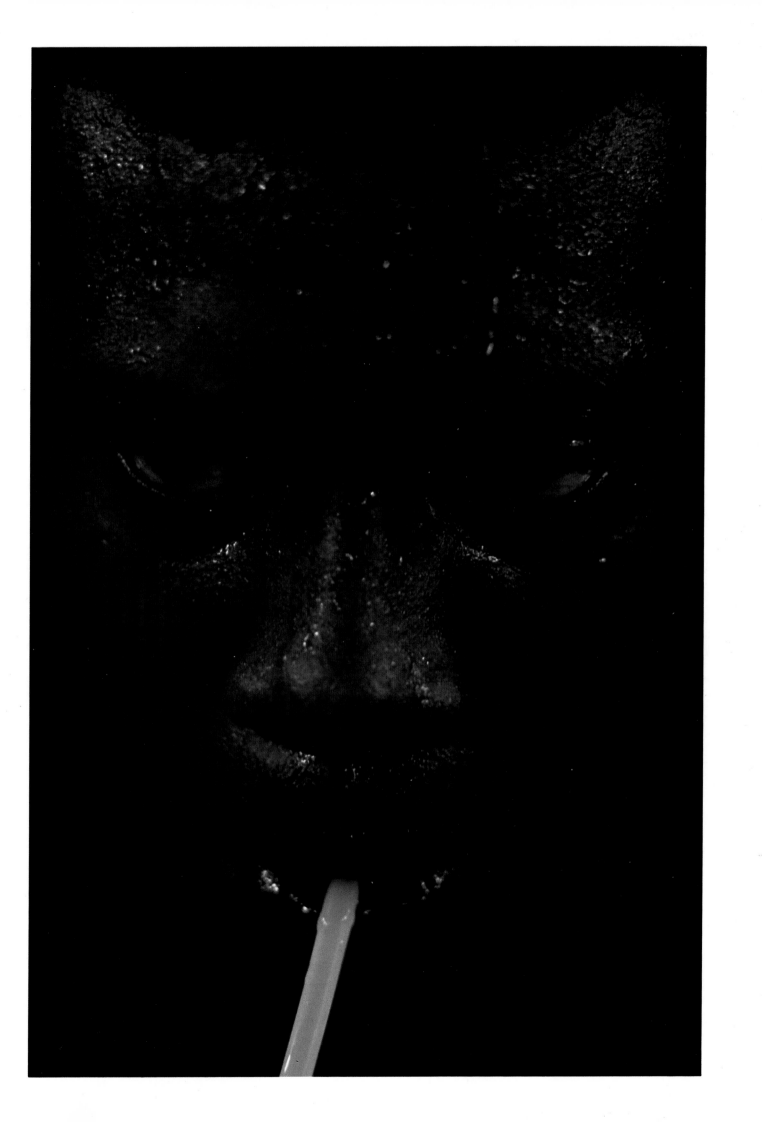

As in my photograph at Denver, I had found another interesting wall. The officials were startled when they realized someone was actually photographing them. 1979. Soldiers Field, Chicago

Part of my Cowboys essay: an experiment in flash. October 1981. Texas Stadium

Steve Grogan takes the field. 1979. Orange Bowl

I walked onto the field at Texas Stadium behind Houston's Earl Campbell. This is against the rules, even during pregame warmup, and I was quickly escorted off by a guard. November 1979

Fans

Opposite: One of the most bizarre sights I've ever witnessed. During halftime at Super Bowl IV an entertainer ignited himself. That's entertainment. January 17, 1970. Tulane Stadium, New Orleans

Following pages: On New Year's Day, 1981, I flew from New Orleans, where I had covered the Sugar Bowl, to Miami, for the Orange Bowl. I made the start of the game. As I circled the field looking for interesting fans, I couldn't help noticing this large teenager. He looked like the son of the wrestler Andre the Giant. He was sitting in the end zone with a group of black bus drivers behind him. This was during a period of racial unrest in Miami, and I wasn't getting a lot of friendly looks. I kept passing him by, unable to bring my camera to my eye, but I had to take this picture to end my torment. I finally approached the boy, who sat mute while the kids around him raised their hands signaling "we're No. 1," meaning Florida State. I asked them to stop, quickly took my few shots, and left. Not until I saw the contact sheet did I realize the looks on the drivers' faces. The heat was on. (Incidentally, Oklahoma won by a point.)

Pages 100–101: Peeping Pedro. While at the Los Angeles Memorial Coliseum making my rounds in search of "the fan," I saw a boy peering under the entrance to the ladies room. October 1980

Pages 102–103: Halftime is a good time to see how the American sports fan is holding up. Here we have "Super Tim," the self-declared biggest fan of the Steelers. Tim was barely holding up: midway through the third period he was unconscious. October 1980. Three Rivers Stadium

Pages 104–105: I met this fan moments after encountering Super Tim. This guy not only had a tattoo of a gun, he had the real thing in an ankle holster. He proudly displayed it to me, and offered me a variety of drugs, which I turned down. All this in a period of five minutes. October 1980. Three Rivers Stadium

Pages 106–107: While keeping track of Super Tim's condition I ran into this bizarre group. Welcome to America. October 1980. Three Rivers Stadium

Pages 108–109: Here's one of my favorite shots. I sensed that the only way to show the solidarity of Navy's fans was to do something with their hats. I went to the upper deck looking about, peered down, and saw the pattern of hats. But something had to happen to make it work. Then, a midshipman turned to give an order of address to his mates, and everything clicked. November 1980. Veterans Stadium

Pages 110–11: Decatur vs. Jacksboro. I once cut a clipping from the Dallas Times Herald *about a noted high school rivalry and kept it in the top drawer of my desk in the Time-Life Building during my staff days at SI. On impulse one day, I called a writer in Texas to find out what was happening in high school football, and casually asked if he knew anything about Jacksboro–Decatur, the game from my clipping. He said the two teams were due to play that night. I flew to Texas, arriving in time to see the game's second half. This scene took place after the game: a victorious halfback and his sweetheart. Jacksboro, Texas*

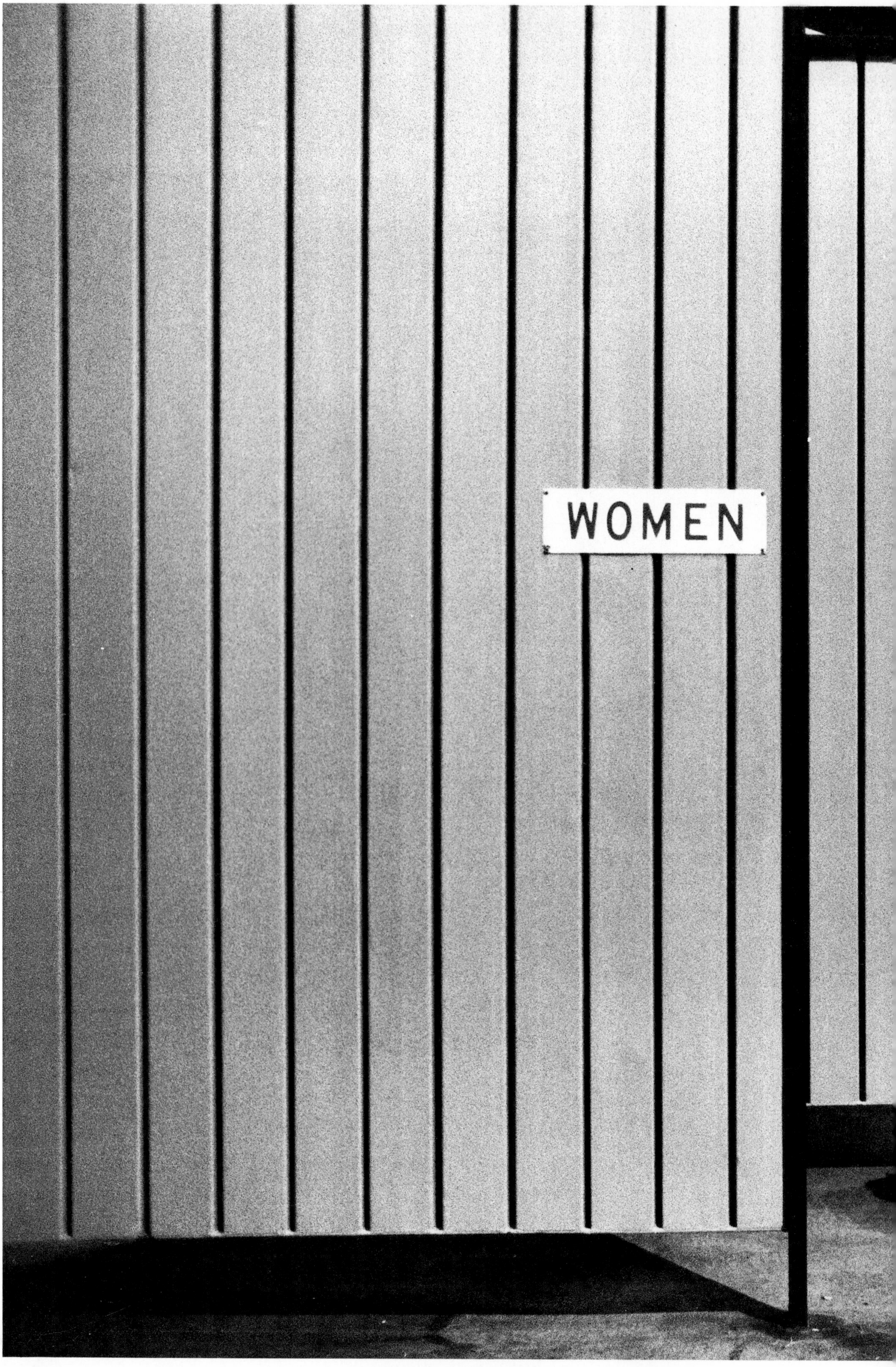
WOMEN

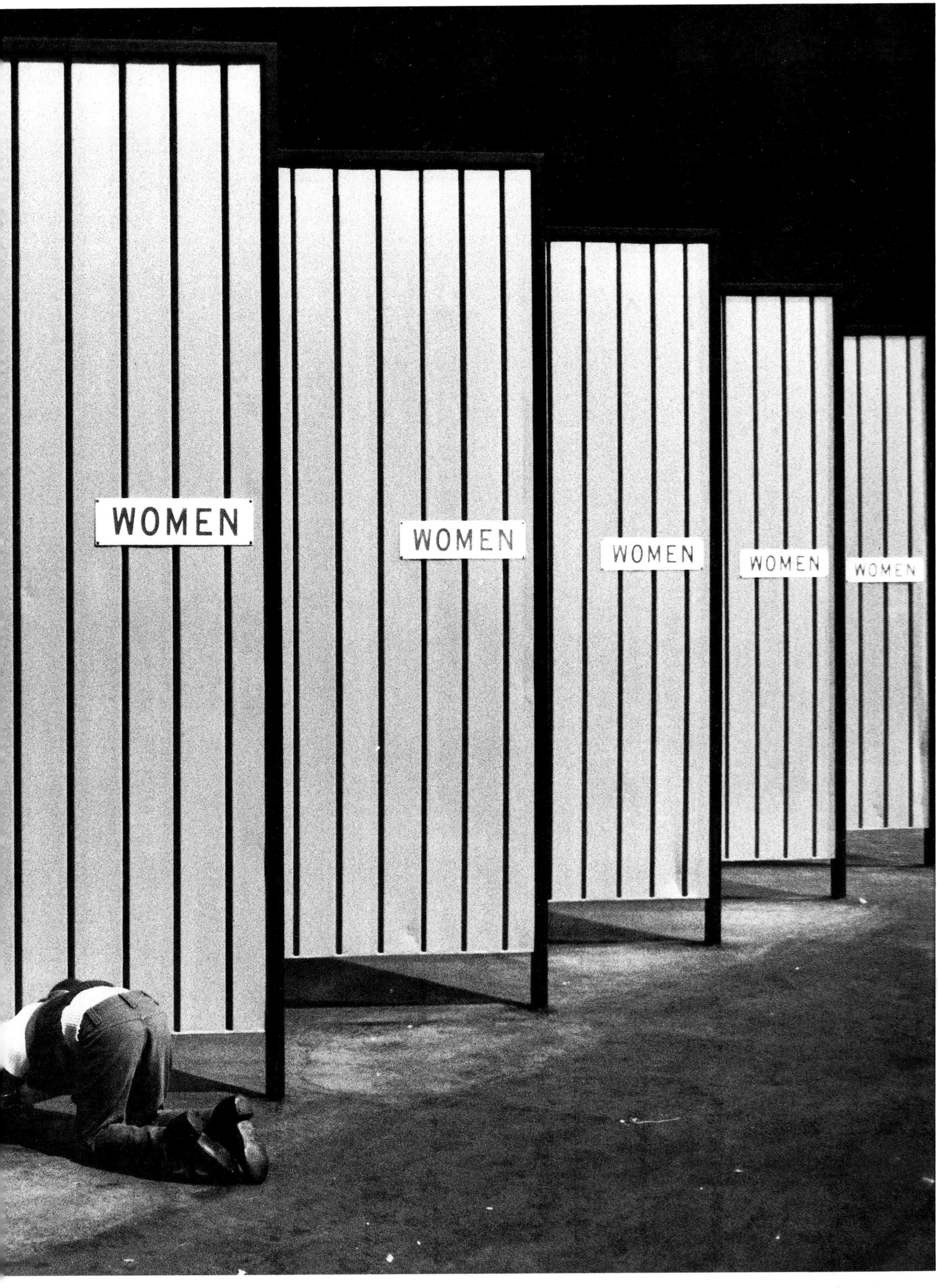

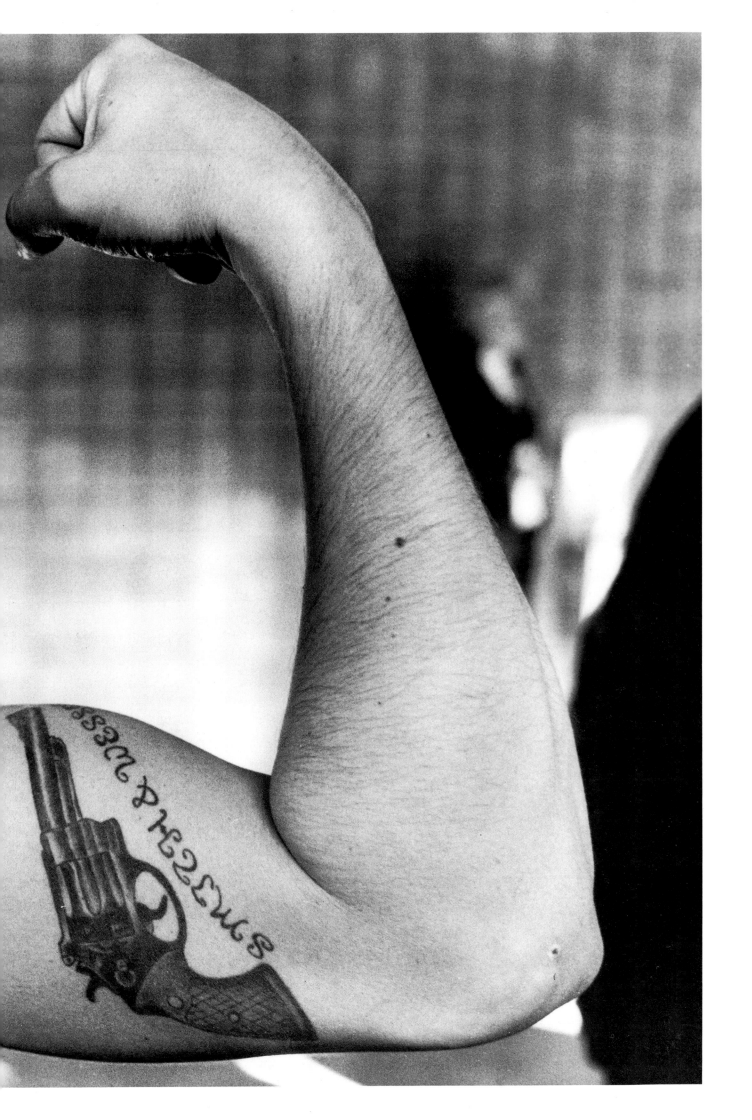

Opposite: A portrait of legendary Pittsburgh quarterback Bobby Layne, one of the last men to play in the NFL without a face mask. October 1962

Sweet Bobby

Bobby Layne was as good at hanging out in bars as he was at throwing passes on the football field. He bragged about it. So the chances are excellent that Sweet Bobby—I think he named himself that—will be more revered for a great philosophical statement he once made than he will for all of the flutter balls he forced into the arms of Doak Walker and his other receivers, or any of the NFL championships he engineered for the Detroit Lions. It was Sweet Bobby who said, "The secret to a happy life is to run out of cash and air at the same time."

Layne was a true competitor and as much of a leader off the field as he was on, which was why so many people other than his faithful teammates sought the pleasure of his company. He liked to close establishments, he could tell good stories, and he always picked up the biggest checks. It was part of his temperament, part of his style. He craved action, he enjoyed good company, and evidently he didn't care much for sleep.

There were those who tried to make a scandal out of a traffic accident he was involved in during the wee hours of a morning in Pittsburgh. (This was after he had been traded from Detroit to the Steelers.)

"What's the big deal?" Bobby said of the collision. "I got hit by a stationary streetcar. It could happen to anybody."

Long before, Layne had been ordained "life's permanent entertainment chairman," as far back as the late 1940s when he was hurling the Texas Longhorns into the Cotton Bowl and the Sugar Bowl. It was a role he accepted with enthusiasm.

Layne understood that he was a legend in his spare time, as they say, and he frequently discussed other quarterbacks the way a legend named Ernest Hemingway discussed other writers and a legend named Frank Sinatra discussed other singers, which was as if they were personal rivals.

"Otto Graham," Layne would say, the words sounding like an epidemic as they rolled off his tongue. "Me and Otto played against each other thirteen times. I could only win twelve of 'em."

Sweet Bobby Layne was not an artistic passer, but he was alarmingly effective. There were times when you felt that his sheer will had forced the ball into a receiver's arms. With Layne's passing and leadership, the Detroit Lions of the 1950s became something of a dynasty on the order of Bart Starr's Packers, Bob Griese's Dolphins, and Terry Bradshaw's Steelers. Sweet Bobby guided the Lions to the NFL Championships of 1952, 1953, and 1957. This didn't surprise Layne. He'd been a winner all his life; he wasn't going to stop in the pros.

Not that he didn't have some help, namely in Doak Walker. Walker, Layne's old high school teammate and collegiate rival, was merely the greatest all-around football player who ever lived. Doak ran, passed, caught, kicked, blocked, and tackled his way to three All-American seasons at SMU, and then he sparkled as an All-Pro in five of his six short years in the NFL. In Detroit, Layne frequently relied on Doak to break the long run or catch the crucial pass.

Layne called Doak a quadruple threat, explaining, "He can run, catch, throw—and win!"

But there were other names on the Lions' roster in those years: Cloyce Box, Lou Creekmur, Joe Schmidt, Bob Hoernschemeyer, Jack Christiansen, Yale Lary, Jim Doran, among them. Together with the names of Layne and Walker, they remind you that the Detroit Lions were once "America's Team."

They entered the realm of folklore in the championship game of December 27, 1953. On that day, the Lions met the Cleveland Browns, who had some household names of their own: Otto Graham, Dante Lavelli, Marion Motley, Lou Groza, among others. In a contest that may have been the best title game ever, the Lions led by 10–3 at the half. Cleveland tied it at 10–10 through the third quarter. The Browns then seized a 16–10 lead on Groza's two field goals in the fourth. This was the score with only two and a half minutes left to play. That was when Sweet Bobby invented the two-minute offense. He sprayed the field with passes, finally nailing Jim Doran with a 33-yard touchdown toss. Doak's extra point (he was also Detroit's kicker) won it for the Lions, 17 to 16.

A broken leg kept Sweet Bobby out of the 1957 title game against Cleveland, but Tobin Rote, his replacement, threw four touchdown passes and wheeled the Lions to this third championship of the Layne era.

"He was afraid not to," Layne said.

Layne was the only person considered for entertainment chairman when Dandy Don Meredith started an annual off-season golf tournament a few years ago for both old and current NFL quarterbacks. Sweet Bobby took the job seriously, immediately instituting a hard and fast rule for the rowdy, four-day weekend: the hospitality suite never closes.

We were in a hotel resort in Hawaii when an incident occurred that told you everything you needed to know about Layne's opinion of the modern-day quarterback crop.

Bobby, myself, and some others were standing out on a hotel balcony one late afternoon, looking down at the lawn where some of Meredith's younger NFL guests were playing catch with a football. Yeah. Pro quarterbacks playing catch. Down there were Dan Pastorini, then with the Houston Oilers, the Vikings' Tommy Kramer, and one or two others.

Somebody yelled down to Pastorini, noted for his strong arm, encouraging him to try to throw the ball up to our balcony. It looked impossible.

But Pastorini flipped the football up to the balcony with ease.

"Jesus," I said to Layne. "He just threw that thing twelve floors up like it was a lateral!"

"Yeah, he did," Layne said calmly. "But his receiver was on the sixth."

You have to understand that to anyone of a certain age who comes from a certain place, Bobby Layne had always been a massive celebrity. He had been a golden-haired, good-looking, tough-as-nails All-State quarterback at Highland Park High in Dallas, and then he had been a golden-haired, good-looking, tough-as-nails All-American quarterback at the University of Texas, and all this was before he had become Sweet Bobby in the pros.

A collegiate image of Layne sticks with me, more so than any other.

In the fall of 1947, Layne's senior year, I had driven down to Austin for the Texas–TCU game. On the morning of the game, I was cruising around the leafy old town and campus when I could have sworn I saw Bobby Layne, only four hours before the kickoff, sitting under an umbrella out in front of a sorority house with two luscious coeds. And of all things, they were sipping champagne out of stemmed glasses.

I once told Layne that I was still in high school at the time, so he could well imagine the impression this scene had made on me: a beautiful autumn morning, and this guy who maybe had to play a football game later on sitting there drinking champagne with these killer-stud home-wreckers. I had always wanted to ask if it had really been him—be serious—in that wondrous mosaic?

"Boy, I was a dumbass in those days," said Sweet Bobby. "When they didn't have any real whiskey, I should have gone somewhere else."

Marino

Super Bowl interviews are among the most absurd things in the world of sport. A player rarely says anything interesting as he sits there uncomfortably before a mass audience. A journalist rarely *asks* anything interesting, seeing as how most of the writers in attendance will either be wretchedly hung over from the night before or individuals who have chosen the wrong profession in the first place. They would have been much happier as publicity flacks.

At Super Bowls, I've gone to these interviews only to collect the dumb questions, maybe, or else look for a journalist friend who had last been seen on Bourbon Street and had been missing for three days.

The questions run along these lines: "Do you expect to have any trouble covering Bob Hayes, the world's fastest human?"

And the responses run along these lines:

"You have asked me if I expect to have any trouble covering Bob Hayes, the world's fastest human. No."

Now and then, a player will evade a question, and this can get the room excited. What can the player be hiding? Even the incompetent senses there might be a story here.

My favorite moment in Super Bowl interviews occurred in a session with Miami's gifted passer, Dan Marino, before the Dolphins were blown away by the San Francisco 49ers in Super Bowl 18. (I don't do Roman numerals.)

Marino likes to act like a cool, laid-back guy. He enjoys winking at cameramen and sitting around with his old high school and college buddies, drinking Iron City beer.

Marino handled the interview with a carefree attitude until somebody asked him why he wore two wrist bands. A quarterback normally only wears a sweat band on his throwing arm. Marino wore one on each wrist.

"That's a dumb question," Marino said, pointing quickly to another writer holding up his hand.

Three questions later, Marino was again asked about the two wrist bands.

"I said that was dumb," he replied. And he pointed to another questioner.

Two more questions were asked that had no bearing on the burning wrist band issue. In the audience, certain writers were beginning to exchange glances, acknowledging to one another that they were on the track of something big. Was the second sweat band covering up a herpes scab on his left wrist? Was the second sweat band disguising a childhood deformity? Was the second sweat band hiding a lurid tattoo?

The writers couldn't stand the suspense. Besides, many of them had deadlines approaching.

From the crowd, a brave writer stood up and pressed the question on Marino again.

"Sorry, Dan, but we have to get to the bottom of this," the writer said. "What's the story on the two wrist bands?"

Gesturing with both hands, and with a trace of impatience in his voice, Marino said:

"It looks good, awwright?"

Miami quarterback Dan Marino hands off to running back Lorenzo Hampton. October 20, 1985.
Orange Bowl

Above: I never felt I made a really good photograph of Jim Brown, but there was no way I could leave him out of the book. In eight of his nine years with the Browns, he led the NFL in rushing. November 1965. Cleveland Stadium

Following pages: This is one of those photographs that looks as if it should have been easy to shoot. But I've tried similar shots countless times and never have made a better picture. December 1979. Giants Stadium, East Rutherford, New Jersey

Opposite: Taken on one of my few visits to Green Bay. Jim Taylor is not posing: it's one of those times when for an instant an athlete lets you look through your lens and into his soul. Lambeau Field, Green Bay, Wisconsin

Above: Super Bowl I. In Jim Taylor's last season with the Packers, his team played in the first AFL–NFL championship game, which Green Bay won over Kansas City, 35–10. Taylor rushed for 53 yards and scored a touchdown. January 15, 1967. Los Angeles Memorial Coliseum

During a game between Pittsburgh and Cleveland, I moved in front of the bench, an area prohibited to photographers, to make this shot of John Jefferson with his goggles. He was the first to wear them. October 1979. Cleveland Stadium

Lester Hayes, or The Judge, as he was called by teammates. I asked Lester to pose after practice for some pictures. The Judge responded, "So be it." I said, "I need you in full uniform." "So be it." July 1984. Los Angeles Raiders training camp

One of my more uncomfortable days in photography: one degree above freezing and pouring.
Fullback Leroy Kelly takes the handoff from Bill Nelson. This was the Eastern Conference playoff and
Cleveland beat the Cowboys, 38–14. December 1969. Cotton Bowl, Dallas

Charley Taylor was the best receiver after he caught the ball that I've ever seen. December 1974.
Los Angeles Memorial Coliseum

This was the last NFL championship game before the title was unified in Super Bowl I. Here, Cleveland tackle Dick Modzelewski leaves the field after the Packers beat the Browns, 23–12. January 1, 1966. Lambeau Field

One of the newer inventions in football is the kicking net. I wanted to photograph Reggie Roby and this was as close as I could ever get to him during a game. September 1985. Orange Bowl

Oakland tackle Henry Lawrence comes back to the bench. October 1977. Mile High Stadium

As I followed the Dolphins during the 1985 season, I asked permission to work behind their bench.
To my delight, I captured this tender moment between running back Woody Bennett (34), rookie
fullback Ron Davenport, guard Roy Foster, and wide receiver Duriel Harris—a rare aspect of a sport
that usually projects something tougher.

Above and below: My favorite player. The best hands I ever saw (one fumble in thirteen seasons). I always wore number 82 whenever I played football. Among many other distinctions, Raymond Berry, now coach for New England, was named as a First Team wide receiver on the 1960–84 AFL–NFL All-Star team. September 15, 1963. Baltimore Memorial Stadium

Opposite: In a playoff game between Miami and Oakland, it looked as if Miami had it in the bag when wide receiver Paul Warfield made this catch against safety Jack Tatum. The Raiders, however, mounted a closing drive, scored a last-second touchdown, and went on to the AFC championship. December 1974. Oakland–Alameda County Coliseum

Above: This game between Dallas and Washington was the roughest, hardest-hitting game I've ever photographed. Redskins running back Larry Brown was helped to the bench four times. He had a welt on his head the size of an egg. Despite his efforts, Dallas won. December 1971. Robert F. Kennedy Memorial Stadium, Washington, D.C.

Opposite: Steeler middle linebacker Jack Lambert, an intense player often battered at game's end; he always gave so much of himself. December 1976. Baltimore Memorial Stadium

I got my first chance to use a new Canon high-speed camera while covering Pittsburgh playing Miami in the 1984 season AFC championship game. If you're in focus, high-speed cameras nearly always catch the action, such as John Stallworth's reception here. But you have to be careful; a whole roll of 36-exposure film can go through the camera in 2.5 seconds. Miami won the game, 45–28. January 6, 1985. Orange Bowl

In Green Bay for the NFL championship game with Dallas, I received a wakeup call at my hotel and was notified that it was 10:00 A.M. and 10 degrees below. By game time it was 13 degrees below, and it was even colder when Bart Starr, with thirteen seconds left to play, plunged one yard for the winning touchdown. It was one of the most miserable days of my life. December 1967. Lambeau Field

Above: The first game I ever photographed in the snow. At game's end I didn't want to leave the field until every player had gone. Number 21 was the last. Riverfront Stadium, Cincinnati

Following pages: I knew that December light cast long shadows at the Los Angeles Memorial Coliseum, so I hired a helicopter, hovered over the action, and shot straight down when the Chargers played the Rams there in 1979. The FAA and security police at the stadium frantically radioed us to get out of there, but I stayed long enough to make this photograph.

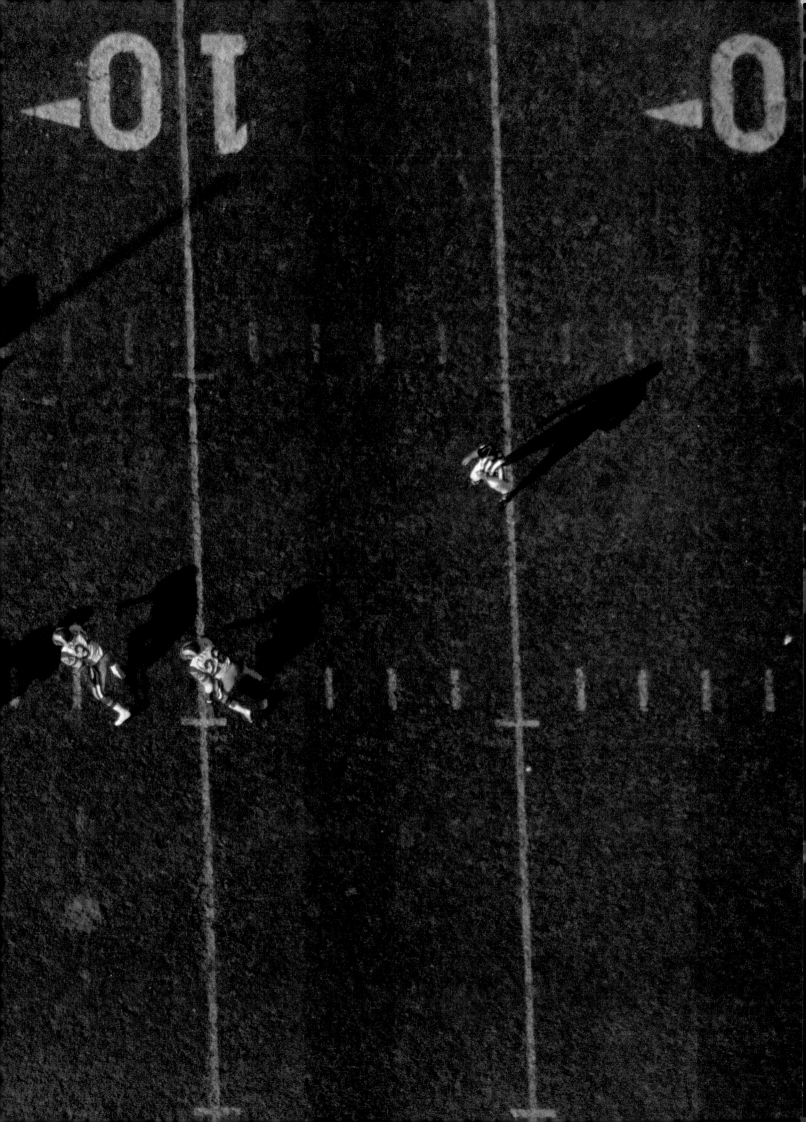

Sonny

Asportswriter can spend an awful lot of his time waiting for celebrity athletes to stop signing autographs. It goes with the territory. Whether at their places of toil—stadiums, ballparks, golf courses, tennis courts, basketball arenas, or in restaurants, bars, airports, shops, or walking down the street, the writer finds himself trying to interrogate the stars through the sometimes constant interruptions of autograph seekers or fans who merely want to shake their hands and tell them how much they've meant to the lives of their children.

Although I had been around far bigger stars over the years, I never saw anybody get the attention that Sonny Jurgensen did when he was throwing touchdown passes for the Washington Redskins.

Maybe Washington, D.C., is—or was—that kind of town. Or maybe Sonny was bigger than I ever realized. He became a close friend so it was hard to think of him as anything other than a fascinating conversationalist and major league drinking companion.

But all I know is that when Sonny went out on the town, he got the heat—the worship, the attention—heat like I had never seen engulf an Arnold Palmer or Jack Nicklaus, a Muhammed Ali, a Johnny Bench, a Jerry West, a Joe Namath, a John McEnroe; hell, even a Howard Cosell.

The redhead handled it well, too. Old Christian Adolph would just stand there chewing on his cigar, or sit there sipping his soda pop, and he'd write something memorable for the autograph seeker, things like:

"You've still got time to make something of yourself. Sonny."

Or:

"Stop tempting fate. Sonny."

Or:

"Kilmer did it. I wasn't even there. Sonny."

Billy Kilmer and Sonny were close friends even though they were continually thrust into the position of having to compete for, and share time at, the Redskins' quarterback job.

If there was anybody who could keep up with Sonny at night, it was Billy. They enjoyed teasing each other unmercifully about their quarterbacking deficiencies, not only around their mutual pals, but often on the sideline during games.

Kilmer came off the field at JFK Stadium one Sunday, bitching, slamming his helmet down, kicking at a water bucket. He had just thrown a ruinous interception.

"No wonder," said Sonny. "It spiraled."

And since Jurgensen never wanted to do anything but throw the ball in a game—and hardly anyone ever threw it better; Sam Baugh, maybe—Kilmer liked to say that Sonny's idea of running the football would be when he couldn't find a receiver open and would have to jog a few steps to avoid Alan Page or somebody.

Kilmer relishes a special moment with Jurgensen. It was in the Redskins' locker room after they had suited up for their first appearance on *Monday Night Football,* a game against the hated Dallas Cowboys.

Sonny and Billy were sitting next to each other on a bench that evening while they and the rest of the squad listened—or pretended to be listening—to Coach George Allen's emotional sermon on the subject of why this game was the most important thing in his own life or all of theirs.

One of the great arms and bellies in pro football. Sonny Jurgensen ended up playing on the Redskins with his pal Billy Kilmer. September 1962. Veterans Stadium

Choked up and teary eyed, Allen finally reached a point in the pregame talk when he made a theatrical gesture.

Allen said, "I'll tell you what this game means to me. I would cut my arm off up to here to win it! Right up to here!"

That was when Jurgensen nudged Kilmer and said in a whisper, "Thank God, it's his left arm. He can still sign checks."

Jurgensen completed something like four hundred million passes in his career, most of them to a couple of receivers named Charley Taylor and Bobby Mitchell. Still, he often liked to joke, "If they'd caught as many as they dropped, there wouldn't be room for anybody else in the record book."

They didn't drop that many, of course, and Sonny was always the first to say that the main reason they *did* drop a ball on occasion was primarily because they both possessed great speed and were overanxious to utilize that speed.

Nevertheless, when Sonny and Bobby Mitchell were inducted into the Pro Football Hall of Fame in Canton, Ohio, a few years ago, Jurgensen had a wisecrack all planned.

He was going to sneak up behind Mitchell when his old Redskin receiver was presented with his plaque, and say:

"Don't drop it, Bobby."

Did Sonny do it? No. Why?

"I didn't throw it," he explained.

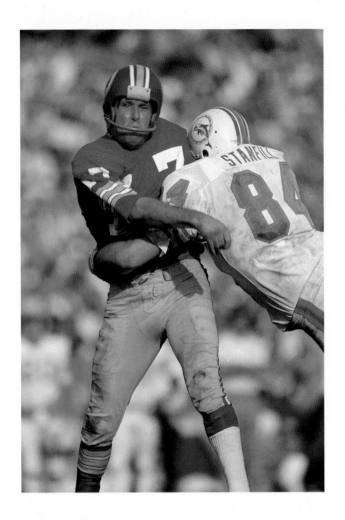

Above left: At Super Bowl VII the day appeared hot and sunny, but smog cut the illumination. Redskins quarterback Billy Kilmer did not seem to enjoy the softer, more beautiful light that resulted. Miami beat Washington, 14–7. January 14, 1973. Los Angeles Memorial Coliseum

Left: This picture was taken when I was still younger than the players. San Diego Chargers tackle Ernie Ladd, at 6' 9", 317 pounds, was one of the biggest people I had ever seen. Ladd later played for Houston and Kansas City, and then turned to pro wrestling. November 10, 1963. Fenway Park, Boston

Above: Close encounters at the Silverdome. This is the most interesting light you'll ever see at an indoor stadium. December 1981. Pontiac Silverdome

Following pages: I made this shot with a 14mm lens, using the roof of the Pontiac Silverdome as the major part of the picture's composition. 1984

Namath

It seems to be against the law of nature for a book to be published on the subject of football without something in it about Joe Namath.

This used to be true of Johnny Unitas and Jim Brown as well, but they didn't play on New York teams. I guess that explains their lack of staying power.

Joe Namath played for the New York Jets after he left the University of Alabama, and above everything else, even his envious ability as a passer, he knew how to *be* a celebrity. That was an imposing combination.

At the peak of his playing career, Joe managed to attract even more attention to himself by wearing white shoes, by living in a Manhattan apartment that was furnished with a white llama rug, and by embracing the nickname of Broadway Joe.

But he got that $427,000 from Sonny Werblen to play for the Jets, and that made him an instant celebrity, and then he won that Super Bowl over the Baltimore Colts, and suddenly Joe Namath was given the unsolicited credit for inventing the American Football League and being solely responsible for its merger with the NFL.

Neither of these last two things was true. Lamar Hunt "made" the American Football League by originating it, and the merger was going to take place anyhow. It made financial sense.

What Namath *did* do was throw the football very well, despite bad knees, and give his team an enormous amount of confidence before the third Super Bowl game by lounging around in the Miami sunshine and saying, "I don't see how Baltimore can win."

This had caused writers to slap their thighs. Baltimore was a 17-point favorite.

But Namath backed up his statement by calling on such friends as Matt Snell, George Sauer, Jr., Don Maynard, and others to help him upset the Colts, 16–7, not that he didn't get a big assist from Baltimore's Earl Morrall, who spent a miserable afternoon overlooking and underthrowing numerous, wide-open Baltimore receivers.

It is seldom written or mentioned these days that Namath's Super Bowl victory didn't entirely gain credibility for the AFL. Many regarded it as a fluke. It wasn't until a year later when the Kansas City Chiefs thrashed the Minnesota Vikings that parity crept into the minds of the press, the public, and the NFL owners.

But Joe Namath had been a big part of it. And football fans are left with this memory of a cool, stoop-shouldered guy who would trot onto the field and make things happen.

I once glorified him in a cover story for *Sports Illustrated,* which couldn't have done anything but enhance his image. I'd spent some time with him in training camp and had sat around with him in a couple of Manhattan bars.

Mostly, I'd observed him watching the door, awaiting the arrival of some shapely adorables, in which case he would say, "Hold it, man. Foxes."

I never heard whether he had liked the story or not, but one evening I ran into a friend of his and couldn't resist asking.

The friend said, "He liked it okay. He doesn't think he says 'man' that much."

Above: New York Jets quarterback Joe Namath held a personal press conference at poolside on Miami Beach before historic Super Bowl III, when the Jets beat the Colts, as Namath had predicted. January 1969

Following pages: On assignment covering Joe Namath in 1975, I borrowed SI's 1,000mm lens, which has tremendous magnifying power but requires critical focus and lots of luck. Shea Stadium, New York

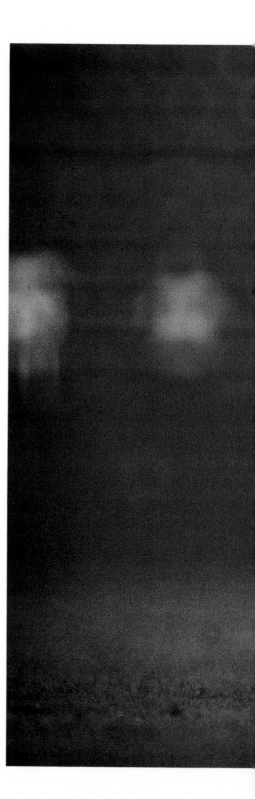

On the sideline covering a Colts game with Buffalo, I was again amazed at the daredevil style of quarterback Bert Jones, who risked injury every time he played. October 1975. Baltimore Memorial Stadium

Above: For an SI essay on violence, I managed to catch Rams tight end Bob Klein being savaged by a defender. September 1975. Los Angeles Memorial Coliseum

Following pages: Oakland's great defensive lineman Otis Sistrunk looked like he had a helmet on all the time because he shaved his head. I made this shot of him hand-fighting Cincinnati tackle Vern Holland. October 1976. Oakland–Alameda County Coliseum

Vikings quarterback Joe Kapp is not calling signals, but is yelling at the referee about the Cleveland defense. Minnesota went on to Super Bowl IV, following their 27–7 victory over the Browns in this NFL championship game. January 4, 1970. Hubert H. Humphrey Metrodome, Minneapolis

The 600mm lens dramatizes the perils of a quarterback. Dallas's Roger Staubach feels the weight of Pittsburgh defensive end L. C. Greenwood. The Steelers defeated the Cowboys, 21–17, in Super Bowl X at Miami's Orange Bowl. January 18, 1976

Redskins quarterback Billy Kilmer watches as Eagles tackle Ernie Calloway manhandles his running back. November 1971. Veterans Stadium

This shot of Oakland running back Mark van Eeghen ran as a cover of SI. December 1977.
Baltimore Memorial Stadium

Above: Pittsburgh right end Dwight White nearly took the head off this Dallas running back and sacked the quarterback three times in Super Bowl X. January 18, 1976. Orange Bowl

Opposite: A few members of the vaunted Steel Curtain defense. Here, Joe Greene (75), L. C. Greenwood (68), and Mel Blount (27) engulf running back Mike Garrett of San Diego. October 3, 1971. Three Rivers Stadium

Following pages: One of the NFL's most intense rivalries of the 1970s developed between Dallas and Washington. I made this shot of Walt Garrison smothered by Redskins defenders Diron Talbert and Manny Sistrunk for a news story in SI. November 21, 1975. Robert F. Kennedy Memorial Stadium

Above: When Pittsburgh wide receiver John Stallworth caught what proved to be the winning touchdown catch in Super Bowl XIV, I was positive not only that I had the shot but that it would make the cover of SI. It's rare I'm so confident of a result. January 20, 1980. Rose Bowl

Opposite: Dwight Clark's amazing catch over Everson Walls won the championship game and enabled San Francisco to go on to win Super Bowl XVI. The photograph capped my efforts to make a great picture with a 50mm lens. I was following quarterback Joe Montana with a 400mm lens. As

Montana released the ball, I saw a receiver break toward me. Cradling the telephoto lens camera in my left arm, I grabbed the other camera hanging around my neck with my right hand, and focused and clicked just as Clark made the catch of his life. January 1982. Candlestick Park, San Francisco

Following pages: A day with great clouds in Cleveland. With time running out, Franco Harris heads for the locker room. As it happens, this was the same day that I made the picture of Franco leaving the locker room reproduced on page 82. October 1979. Cleveland Stadium

Above: Cornerback Mel Renfro feels the pain moments after Baltimore's Jim O'Brien kicked a winning field goal with five seconds left to beat Dallas in Super Bowl V. January 17, 1971. Orange Bowl

Opposite: At Super Bowl IV I caught Kansas City head coach Hank Stram congratulating quarterback Len Dawson before the game was over. I could have been kicked out of the stadium for stepping on the field, but the crowd was giving Dawson (later named the game's MVP) a big ovation for his winning performance against Minnesota, and nobody noticed me. January 11, 1970. Tulane Stadium

Above: A pair of tackles. Oakland's Bob Brown is probably thinking about a hot shower as a young fan takes a souvenir from a smiling Mean Joe Greene. 1973. Oakland—Alameda County Coliseum

Opposite: A foggy day. Colts defensive end Bubba Smith leaves the field after Baltimore took the AFC championship from Oakland, Smith having forced quarterback Daryle Lamonica to leave the game in the second quarter. January 1971. Baltimore Memorial Stadium

After the 1976 AFC playoff game against Pittsburgh, Johnny Unitas, the defeated Colts quarterback, leaves the field. December 1976. Baltimore Memorial Stadium

After Super Bowl XVIII I found this shot of defensive tackle Bruce Davis in my boxes of pictures that SI had rejected. January 22, 1984. Tampa Stadium

Lombardi

Jerry Kramer once said of Vince Lombardi: "He's a cruel, kind, tough, gentle, miserable, wonderful man whom I often hate and often love but always respect."

I could personally testify to the cruel, tough, miserable part. Lombardi made my job hard.

In 1964, in one of those rare seasons when Lombardi lost the NFL championship, I was sent out to Green Bay to do a cover piece on the Packers for *Sports Illustrated.*

I informed the coach I was coming out there for an interview. He said fine. So I flew in a blizzard to Chicago, then drove in a blizzard to Green Bay. In yet another blizzard I went over to the Packers' offices the next morning.

For the next six hours I sat in Lombardi's outer office. Nobody offered coffee. Nobody told me where the Coke machine was. Nobody invited me to look at game films. Nobody was willing to chat. Everybody was *afraid* to chat.

I was finally shown into Vince's office where we visited for about thirty minutes. It was a half hour of evasion, as I saw it.

The only thing that saved the trip—and my story—was the evening I spent in Green Bay with Paul Hornung and Max McGee, two friends who would even tell me some stories I could print, and who were more than adept at finding whatever fun there was to be had in Green Bay in the evenings.

I wrote a generally favorable story about the Packers, no thanks to Lombardi, with the possible exception of a few lines in which I said things like there is probably nothing wrong with the Packers that Vince can't fix by growling a lot.

Then Lombardi became a God and I became a seminovelist.

Cut to a few years later when Lombardi and I both wound up in the same saloon in New York City. It was P. J. Clarke's, in fact.

Lombardi's entrance had been greeted with applause by the other customers. Mine had been greeted by a waiter who handed me a check I'd forgotten to pay the night before.

We sat at different tables on opposite sides of the back room with our own friends. But somewhere along the way, Lombardi spotted me and motioned for me to come over and have a cocktail with him.

I did. And in the course of the next hour, after hearing the kind of football stories I wished I had heard all those years before, I reminded him of the time I'd gone out to Green Bay to interview him.

"You kept me waiting for six hours," I said.

He claimed he didn't remember it.

"No coffee," I said. "Nothing."

"I couldn't have done that," he said with a gap-tooth smile.

"You did," I insisted.

"Wait a minute," he said. "What year are we talking about?"

"Nineteen sixty-four," I said.

He thought a minute.

"Yes," he said. "It might have happened. In those days I had some problems with the office staff. They probably didn't tell you were there."

I laughed. I clinked my glass against his. All Gods have a right to revise history.

Green Bay coach Vince Lombardi leaves the field after his Packers defeated the Baltimore Colts, 13–10, in a sudden death Western Conference playoff game. Even in victory Lombardi's intensity always made me nervous, and the 35mm lens got me about as close to him as I wanted to be. December 26, 1965. Lambeau Field

The patience of fans is both endless and as brief as a blink, depending upon whether you have won or lost for them.

Above: During my season covering the Steelers, and after a particularly bad loss to Cleveland, I found Coach Chuck Noll holding his postgame interview in appropriately depressing surroundings. October 1979. Cleveland Stadium

Following page: The bottom line of this picture is that all football players want the same thing—to wear a Super Bowl ring. July 1984. Los Angeles Raiders training camp

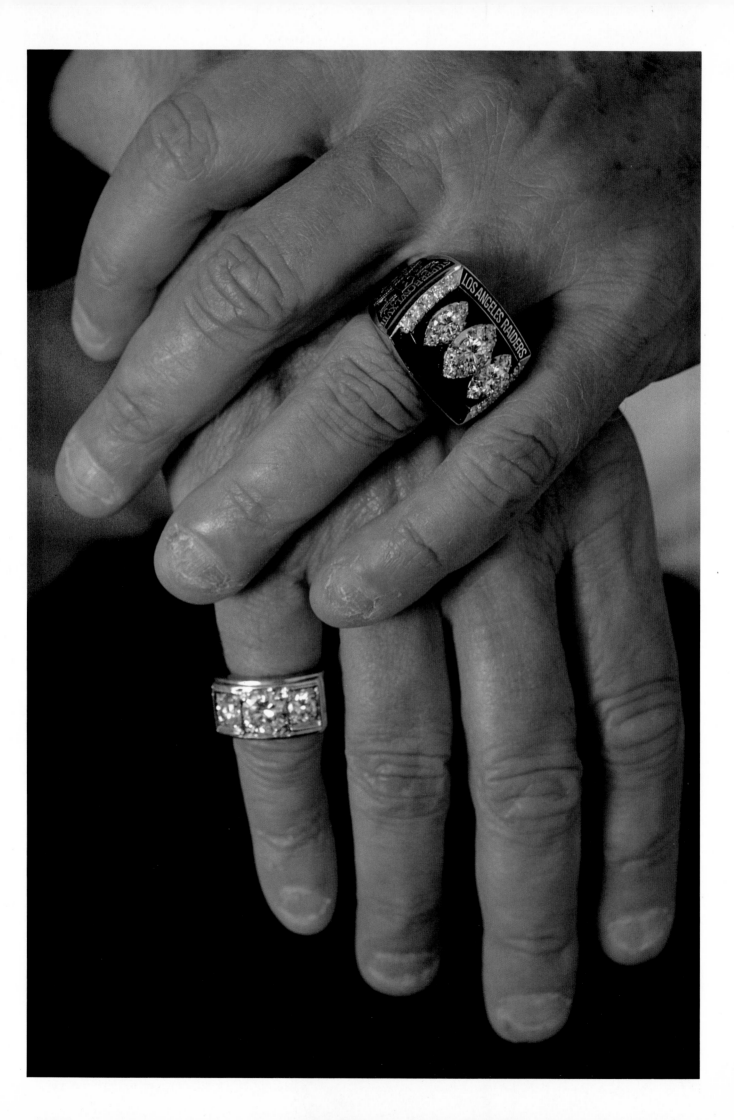